Twayne's United States Authors Series

Sylvia E. Bowman, *Editor*

INDIANA UNIVERSITY

William Inge

WILLIAM INGE

by

R. BAIRD SHUMAN

The first playwright to deal seriously with America's Midwestern heartland, William Inge has the unique distinction of having produced four consecutive Broadway successes in ten years. *Come Back, Little Sheba*, his first hit, was followed by the Pulitzer Prize-winning *Picnic*, by *Bus Stop*, and *The Dark at the Top of the Stairs*. Appreciated by critics and public alike, all of these plays are characterized by Inge's probing of the loneliness, isolation, insecurity, and psychological complexity of seemingly humdrum people.

Though his "Golden Decade" has been followed by a falling off of critical and popular esteem, Inge remains perhaps the most convincing Realist in the American drama. This study reveals him as a playwright who, at his frequent best, has written with a power and veracity that have placed him with Tennessee Williams and Arthur Miller as the three most potent forces in the mid-century American drama.

WILLIAM INGE

By R. BAIRD SHUMAN

Duke University

 95

Twayne Publishers, Inc.   ::   New York

For two far-sighted historians

WILLIAM H. CARTWRIGHT, JR.
and
ROBERT ALLEN NYE

Preface

WILLIAM INGE'S first permanent job was in teaching. For one year he taught high school English, and for eight years he taught English and drama in college. However, through all of this period, his heart was really in the theater; and, as soon as the Theatre Guild offered him its option on *Come Back, Little Sheba* (1950), he resigned his instructorship at St. Louis' Washington University to move to New York. The decade which followed was filled with years of heady success when the author was awarded the Pulitzer Prize in Drama; when he saw four successive productions of his plays win wide acclaim, both critical and popular; and when he came to be considered one of America's three greatest contemporary dramatists.

The new decade has been less encouraging to Inge than the one immediately preceding it. His only success since 1959 has been his scenario, *Splendor in the Grass*. The critical reception of *A Loss of Roses* was sufficiently unfavorable to cause the author to leave New York for a time, during which he produced the scenario. He did the writing for two other films, *All Fall Down*, which was entered in the Cannes Film Contest, and *That Hill Girl*. He also readied a new play for production, but *Natural Affection* was to receive even harsher critical treatment than had been accorded *A Loss of Roses*.

In an interview which he gave to *Newsweek* magazine (May 14, 1962, 110) shortly after *Natural Affection* had been poorly received on the road, Inge is quoted as having said: "I'm somewhat angrier than I used to be, but, oddly enough, more contented, too. . . . I like to be near UCLA, where I've been talking to classes in the Theatre Arts. I suspect I may end up as a teacher." If his suspicion comes to pass, Inge will have come full circle in fifteen years. However, the author is now back in New York working on a new play, and he is likely to remain a force in American theater for some years to come.

This volume represents the first, full-length critical consideration of Inge's work. It deals with all of his plays from 1947 to 1963: *Farther Off From Heaven* to *Natural Affection*. *Splendor in the Grass* is considered as well in an attempt to demonstrate Inge's use of a new, more flexible medium. I chose to deal with this scenario rather than with one of the other two because *Splendor in the Grass*, published in book form, is easily available to readers.

Inge's biography is dealt with in Chapter One, primarily as it concerns his work and his artistic development. Chapter Two deals with four notable successes: *Come Back, Little Sheba; Picnic; Bus Stop;* and *The Dark at the Top of the Stairs.* These plays are considered separately in chronological order and are discussed in a single chapter not only because they were all successful, but also because they bear a thematic, technical kinship to one another. Chapter Three deals with the fifth and sixth Inge plays to be produced on Broadway—*A Loss of Roses* and *Natural Affection*—and with *Splendor in the Grass* which is a product of the same period as Inge's two commercial failures.

Chapter Four is devoted to a consideration of Inge's shorter plays with the exception of *People in the Wind* which is discussed with *Bus Stop* for which it provided the basis, just as the full length *Summer Brave* is discussed with *Picnic*, a different version of the same play. Chapter Five is devoted to general conclusions about Inge and his work.

Farther Off From Heaven is not dealt with in great detail because the play is not available in printed form, an omission which hopefully will be remedied in time. This play, which provided the basis for *The Dark at the Top of the Stairs*, contains a great deal of material which is essentially autobiographical, and for that reason alone it would be helpful to have available a published version. Inge's first major television play, *Out on the Outskirts of Town* (1964), is not discussed because it was produced after the completion of this study, as was the Inge film *Bus Riley's Back in Town* (1965).

I have also been unable to obtain a copy of *Front Porch*, Inge's second play, of which *Picnic* and *Summer Brave* are reworkings. There has been no production of *Front Porch* under the title, nor has the play been published. Presumably it is virtually identical to *Picnic*, although somewhat less unified than the Pulitzer Prize play.

R. Baird Shuman

Yuma, Arizona

Acknowledgments

The writer's major debt of gratitude is to William Inge whose cooperation has been most gratifying. Professor Sylvia Bowman has been an understanding editor who has approached her work in editing this volume with admirable intelligence and dispatch.

The Duke University Council on Research provided the writer with funds which made it possible for him to pursue his research with an intensity which would otherwise have been impossible.

The staffs of the Duke University Library, the Stanford University Library, the Libraries of the University of California at Berkeley, Santa Barbara, and Los Angeles, the University of Southern California Library, the University of Texas Library, the San José State College Library, the University of North Carolina Library, and the Library of the George Peabody College for Teachers are deeply in the writer's debt for their assistance.

Discussions of Inge and of the present volume have been of significant assistance to the writer, and for critical insights he is indebted to H. Charles Hutchings II of the University of California Medical School at Los Angeles and to Paul and Elizabeth Green of Chapel Hill.

Finally, to his colleagues at Duke University in both the Department of Education and the Department of English, the author owes considerable gratitude for their continuing encouragement and interest.

Contents

Chronology

1913 William Motter Inge born in Independence, Kansas, May 3, the fifth and last child of Maude Sarah Gibson and Luther Clayton Inge.

1927- Attended Montgomery County High School, Independ-
1930 ence, Kansas.

1930- Attended the University of Kansas. Received the A. B. in
1935 1935.

1932 Acted in a Kansas tent show during the summer.

1933 Worked with the summer theater sponsored by Culver Military Academy.

1935- Attended George Peabody College for Teachers and left
1936 two weeks before graduation because of illness.

1936 Spent summer working on a road gang in Kansas.

1936- Was a news announcer for radio station KFH, Wichita,
1937 Kansas.

1937- Taught English in the Columbus, Kansas, high school.
1938

1938 Completed work for the A. M. in English during the summer and was awarded the degree. His thesis was entitled *David Belasco and the Age of Photographic Realism in the American Theatre.*

1938- Taught English composition and drama at Stephens Col-
1943 lege, Columbia, Missouri.

1943- Employed as art, music, book, and drama critic for the St.
1946 Louis *Star-Times.*

1945 Met Tennessee Williams; wrote his first play, *Farther Off From Heaven.*

1946- Taught English at Washington University, St. Louis,
1949 Missouri.

1947 *Farther Off From Heaven* produced by Margo Jones's Little Theatre Group in Dallas, Texas.

1949 *Come Back, Little Sheba* given a tryout by the Theatre Guild in Westport, Connecticut.

1950 *Come Back, Little Sheba* produced on Broadway.

1953 *Picnic* produced on Broadway. Author awarded Pulitzer Prize in Drama, Drama Critics' Circle Award, and Donaldson Award. Outer Critics' Circle voted *Picnic* the best play of the year.

1955 *Bus Stop* produced on Broadway.

1957 *The Dark at the Top of the Stairs* produced on Broadway.

1959 *A Loss of Roses* produced on Broadway; *Four Plays by William Inge* published by Random House.

1961 *Splendor in the Grass* produced.

1962 *Summer Brave and Eleven Short Plays* published by Random House.

1963 *Natural Affection* produced on Broadway.

1964 *Out on the Outskirts of Town* produced on national television network.

1965 Screen version of *Bus Riley's Back in Town.*

William Inge

CHAPTER 1

From Deep Within the Heartland

AMERICA'S HEARTLAND—the Midwest—has not been ignored by the creators of American literature. Theodore Dreiser, in *Sister Carrie* and in *Jennie Gerhardt*, chronicled the stories of two women who bolted from the heartland in desperation and attempted to make lives for themselves in metropolitan Chicago. Edgar Lee Masters recounted in poetry the stories of townsfolk resting in a cemetery on the hill above Spoon River. Willa Cather told of the pioneers who homesteaded in Nebraska. Sinclair Lewis exposed the philistinism of Gopher Prairie and Zenith. Sherwood Anderson wrote of the hypocrisy and frustration of people at the eastern extreme of America's heartland. Carl Sandburg celebrated Chicago, hog butcher for the world.

Nevertheless, despite the literary attention which the heartland has received, the writers of drama who turned their skills to a portrayal of Midwestern America—and there have been notably few of these—celebrated mostly the wholesomeness of the area. The most celebrated musical comedy of the 1940's, *Oklahoma!*, is set in the same general area as many of William Inge's plays; yet, as Robert Brustein has noted, Rodgers and Hammerstein's Oklahoma is "a joyous zone of calico gowns, scrubbed blue jeans, and homogenized souls."[1] Midwesterners came to be stereotyped in drama as a hearty breed of milkmaids and cowpokes or, in plays like Meredith Willson's *The Music Man*, as people associated with "brass bands, 'Ioway stubbornness,' and ingratiating con-men."[2]

William Inge may justifiably be called the first playwright to examine the Midwest with insight and to write seriously of it—

to have concern for the sociological uniqueness of the area and for the psychological manifestations of this uniqueness as it is revealed in the reactions of its people. Inge has presented with astounding veracity the oppressive banality of the lives of his characters. The events of their lives have the nerve-tightening regularity of a dripping faucet. His female characters especially are engulfed by the bathos of their lives, and Inge capitalizes on this fact in order to heighten dramatically the moment of personal crisis which comes to each of them. In each of his four major successes—*Come Back, Little Sheba; Picnic; Bus Stop;* and *The Dark at the Top of the Stairs*—the play carries the audience through the moment of crisis; and the final curtain falls upon a note of hope and fulfillment. And, except in the case of Madge in the stage version of *Picnic*, this hope and fulfillment come as a result of an acceptance of reality, an adjustment to inevitability, and a willingness to face life on non-romantic terms.

I *The Long Wait*

Born in Independence, Kansas, in 1913, William Inge was to wait thirty-two years before he wrote his first play and thirty-four years before he saw the first production of his work in Margo Jones's Theatre '47 in Dallas. William, the youngest of five children of Maude Sarah Gibson and Luther Clayton Inge, showed an early interest in theatrics. When he was eight years old, he learned a recitation which his sister Helene had been rehearsing; and one day he jumped up in school and blurted out:

> Hi-yo, Peter Johnson,
> Come inside that fence;
> I done told yo' yesterday
> Yo' ain't got no sense.

This display delighted his classmates; and Inge, reflecting on this incident, later wrote: "For the first time I felt that audience reaction. It meant an awful lot to me. I hadn't been a very good student at all. From then on I found a way of getting on with people that I hadn't [previously] had."[3]

At about this time young Bill Inge also became an avid collector of pictures of silent film stars and often, like Sonny in *The Dark at the Top of the Stairs,* found in these pictures an escape from the dull reality through which he was living. Also like Sonny, Inge was closer to his mother than to his father whose job as a traveling salesman kept him away from his home and family a great deal. This close contact with his mother was instrumental in helping Inge to understand the mother-son relationships which he was later to write about with such feeling and perception. The play in which Inge draws most directly from his own past, *The Dark at the Top of the Stairs,* while not completely autobiographical, represents the author's coming to grips with many of the fundamental psychological problems which faced him during adolescence and early adulthood. Inge calls *The Dark at the Top of the Stairs* "my first cautious attempt to look at the past, with an effort to find order and meaning in experiences that were once too close to be seen clearly."⁴ The first version of this play, *Farther Off From Heaven,* was, according to the author, "a sort of sketch—something I wanted to do in deeper perspective."⁵ It was not until he had undergone extensive psychoanalytical treatment, however, that he was able to achieve the deeper perspective which is evident in his finished product, *The Dark at the Top of the Stairs.*⁶ By the time he had transformed *Farther Off From Heaven* into this play, Inge had stood back dispassionately and viewed himself. The play is not strictly autobiographical because it generalizes more fully than does consciously contrived autobiography; it is, rather, a psychological collage, the essence of which is found in the author's past.

Inge's boyhood in Independence was not significantly different from that of any other average boy growing up in the Midwest during the 1920's, except, perhaps, that he was a bit more sensitive and a bit more introspective than were many of his peers. Being the youngest of five children, he was more protected than the average child. He early became a good listener and a shrewd observer of people, qualities which were to prove invaluable assets to him when he began to write plays.

Inge, who even in elementary school had been an amateur monologuist, entered Montgomery County High School in Independence in 1927 and soon became involved in school dramatic productions. Theater intrigued him, and with his uncle, a frustrated Thespian, he sometimes attended the plays which road companies brought to Kansas City. When, after his graduation from high school in 1930, he entered the University of Kansas, Inge continued to be active in theatrical groups; and during two college summers he toured with a Toby show, playing juvenile roles.[7] He came to look upon the day when he would be graduated from college as the day of liberation when he would finally go to New York to pursue his acting ambitions. He was especially determined that the theater should be his life after spending the summer of 1933 working with the summer theater group sponsored by Culver Military Academy. However, when Inge received his bachelor of arts degree in 1935, he, like many college graduates during the Depression, found himself virtually without funds and without prospects. He could see no possible means of going to New York; and, when he was offered a scholarship to attend George Peabody College for Teachers in Nashville, he had no choice but to accept the offer and to begin work on a master's degree.

During the early days at Peabody, Inge's heart was a thousand miles away in New York, and the conflict between what he was doing and what he felt convinced he should be doing almost overwhelmed him. It was not long before he suffered a severe nervous reaction which he has since explained by saying, "I sort of based my life on the theatre . . . Having given up the theatre [to go to Peabody], I had given up the basis I'd set my life upon. I was terribly miserable and confused. I went home to Kansas and began to flounder."[8] This floundering, while intensely painful to the author, was probably very valuable to him; for it forced him to consider in a more clearly defined manner than ever before the purpose of his life and the course that it should take. As he began to work toward a better understanding of his problems, he found physical exhaustion helpful; and, during the summer of 1936 when he was a laborer for the Kansas State Highway Department, he worked vigorously for long hours in the summer heat. By autumn he had regained a great deal of his physical and mental tone. The theater was still foremost in his mind, and he now took a job as an announcer for radio station KFH in Wichita. He had temporarily put from his mind the thought of pursuing an acting career.

And now, apparently, a change took place in Inge. He had always had confidence when he appeared before audiences; he had never been bothered by stage fright or self-consciousness. However, when he played the role of the choir master in an amateur performance of Thornton Wilder's *Our Town* in 1938, he reported, "Suddenly I found I was terrified, too self-conscious to ever act again."[9] In a sense this experience marked Inge's emancipation from a dream which had prevented him from finding his real course in life, but it took him seven more years to find his true direction. Meanwhile, he temporized; but he temporized meaningfully; and, had he carefully planned the next seven years as a means of achieving his ultimate goal, they could not have provided a better preparation for his eventual emergence as a playwright.

II *And Gladly Teche*

By June, 1937, Inge had completed most of the work for his master's degree at Peabody. He still had to write a thesis; but he had for a year been free of course work which would require his presence on campus. He accepted a position as a teacher of English in the high school of Columbus, Kansas. After a year there, he became a member of the faculty at Stephens College for Women in Columbia, Missouri. He taught some freshman composition; but he was most directly involved in the teaching of drama and in the production of plays. Inge remained at Stephens for five years and found especially rewarding his contacts with his colleague, Maude Adams, whose enthusiasm for theater matched his own and whose intelligence and experience he greatly admired.

Had it not been for World War II, Inge might well have remained at Stephens and might never have become a playwright. However, he interrupted his teaching career from 1943 to 1946 to join the staff of the St. Louis *Star-Times* to fill the demanding job of music, art, book, and drama critic, a position left vacant when its previous occupant was drafted. Inge realized that this post had to be held open for his predecessor; he knew that, in leaving the security of Stephens College, he faced the possibility of competing for positions with a deluge of veterans at the war's end. But he could not permit the desire for security to stand in his way when he had the opportunity of being a professional drama critic. And it was this position which served as the catapult to Inge's career as playwright. Even though he left the *Star-Times* in 1946 and became for three years instructor of English at Washington University in St. Louis, the turning point in his life had been reached.

Inge had done little writing until 1945. He had struggled through his master's thesis, *David Belasco and the Age of Photographic Realism in the American Theatre,* and had received the master's degree in 1938. However, he had done little creative work beyond a few fragmentary sketches; indeed, he seemed to be intimidated by the thought of writing creatively. Then, in January, 1945, Tennessee Williams, having had his first taste of success with the Chicago opening of *The Glass Menagerie,* came to St. Louis to recover from the first shock of acclaim in the privacy of his parents' modest suburban home. Inge decided to do a feature article about Williams who was still not well known. Also, as Williams writes, Inge wondered "if I would not enjoy a little social diversion other than that provided by family friends in St. Louis, since my own small group of past associates in the city had scattered far and wide, by this time, like fugitives from a sanguinary overthrow of state."[10] Williams and Inge became acquainted in this way and have been close friends ever since.

Shortly after Williams had returned to Chicago to do further work on *The Glass Menagerie,* Inge went to the city to see the play with Williams. After he had seen the performance, deeply moved by what he called "the finest thing I'd seen in the theatre in years,"[11] he confided to Williams that he wanted to be a playwright.[12] Williams was not entirely sure that Inge was serious in this desire; however, Inge recalls that "I went back to St. Louis and felt, 'Well, I've got to write a play.' "[13] And within three months he had done so. He sent *Farther Off From Heaven* to Williams as soon as he had finished it. Williams, who had just completed arrangements with Margo Jones for the production of *Summer and Smoke* in her Theatre '47 in Dallas, showed Miss Jones the Inge play, which she agreed to produce in the summer of 1947. Inge, in Dallas for the opening, realized that he had discovered his destiny. He returned to Washington University in the fall with the firm conviction that a career in drama lay before him, and soon he had begun serious work on turning a fragmentary short story into a one-act play.

III   *Snips and Snails and Lost Puppy Dogs*

By the beginning of 1949, the one-act play which Inge had intended to write about Lola and Doc had blossomed into a full-length, two-act play in six scenes. *Come Back, Little Sheba* seemed to Inge a great improvement over *Farther Off From Heaven* which he felt "didn't dig very deeply into people's lives, [but] suggested the deeper meaning pretty tentatively."[14] Williams had somewhat earlier interested his agent, Audrey Wood, in Inge's work, and it was to Miss Wood that Inge sent his new play upon its completion. Miss Wood expressed confidence in the play; and on February 4, 1949, she submitted the script to the Theatre Guild. Within four days she had the following preliminary report from the Guild: "A play that at first seems to be almost nothing. But then it grows on you by its little touches and its effects gained by indirection until, by the end, you are genuinely moved. It is impossible to convey in a report the little touches of pity and understanding that make up the texture of this play. In a sense it illustrates Thoreau's 'All men lead lives of quiet desperation.' "[15]

Inge was to spend an anxious year waiting for *Come Back, Little Sheba* to arrive on Broadway. He was still teaching at Washington University when the Theatre Guild optioned the play in the middle of March, 1949. The Equity reading of the play was held on April 5, 1949, and the reaction was so favorable that Inge decided to leave his teaching and to go to New York to oversee the production of his drama. The play was presented before its first audience on September 12, 1949, when it opened in Westport, Connecticut, with Shirley Booth in the leading role. The audience was enthusiastic beyond Inge's most sanguine expectations, and both cast and author received a prolonged ovation at the final curtain. The Westport run was brief, but the play was performed before full houses even though the summer season was actually over.

On September 19, when the play had completed its week in Westport, the Theatre Guild and the author had to reach a crucial decision. Both were eager to see the play on Broadway; but Miss Booth, whose Lola still is credited with being one of the finest performances in American theater, had agreed to appear in another Broadway play which was to open shortly. If *Come Back, Little Sheba* were to be presented during the fall season, it would have to be with someone other than Miss Booth in the lead. The Theatre Guild was reluctant to take the risk; and Inge, restless though he was to know how exacting New York audiences would react to his presentation, agreed that the play would have to be withheld from Broadway until Miss Booth was free to act in it. Drinking huge quantities of coffee, Inge lived on tenterhooks and was virtually unable to proceed with any other projects until the beginning of the new year. *Come Back, Little Sheba* went into rehearsals with its Broadway company on January 2, 1950; it opened in Wilmington on January 26 and moved to Boston four days later. The reviews of the pre-Broadway performances were mixed; however, nearly all of the critics made some favorable comment. Those who did not consider Inge a brilliant playwright had to concede that he was extremely competent and that he was a new playwright of considerable promise.

The culmination of all that Inge had been working for came when *Come Back, Little Sheba* opened at the Booth Theatre in New York on February 15, 1950. Miss Booth and her supporting cast were superb in the first Broadway performance. The critics were generally favorable in their comments about the play, although they all had some significant reservations similar to those of Brooks Atkinson of the New York *Times* who called the play artfully planned, but tight and narrow. A small group of critics was scathing in its comments, but the play was assured of a considerable following.

The play was presented before full houses for the first few weeks of its run of slightly less than six months. After that, as Inge has written, "houses began to dwindle to the size of tea parties."[16] The actors took a cut in salary, and Inge took a smaller royalty in order to keep the play on the boards. Nevertheless, for a first play, *Come Back, Little Sheba* was a success.

It received four votes for the Drama Critics' Circle best play of the 1949-50 season. Shortly before it closed on July 29, 1950, after 190 performances, the play was sold to the films; and this sale assured a profit to its backers. *The Theatre Guild on the Air* also did a version of the play on radio, and the Guild was so well satisfied with Inge that on October 1, 1950, it gave him its option on his next play.

Inge was not unmindful of the hazards which face an author whose career begins too propitiously. He began to feel a growing insecurity, a type of artistic uncertainty as *Come Back, Little Sheba* neared the end of its run. Less than a week before the last performance of the play he wrote, "We are being unfair to a writer if we expect him always to equal our conception of what is his best. Then we set a standard for him and tend to deprive him of his freedom." He goes on to say that "[modern] culture ceases to serve us as a means of identification, it loses its personal value and we tend to make of it a mass experience like a bullfight or a convention."[17] Many new playwrights have to slink off and lick their wounds; but Inge had to face the greater problem of meeting a standard which he had set and an image which many cognoscenti of the theater had now formed of him.

Between the writing of *Farther Off From Heaven* and *Come Back, Little Sheba,* Inge had written a play which was tentatively entitled *Front Porch.* Its basic theme intrigued him, and he now turned to the task of redrafting this somewhat inchoate version of the play which, presented under the new title *Picnic,* was to bring him the Pulitzer Prize, the New York Drama Critics' Circle Award, and the Donaldson Prize in 1953.

When Inge began to rework *Front Porch* in the summer of 1950, he wished to escape from what he called the "gloomy interior . . . and singular melancholy of *Sheba.*"[18] He wanted to write a play which took place in the sunshine, as much of *Picnic* does. The play, which he considered entitling *Women in Summer,* began essentially as a series of dramatic sketches about women, and from this gallery of women Inge had to create his drama. He grappled only briefly with the problem of giving dramatic intensity to his work. He says, "It was instinct on my part to bring into their midst a young man."[19] From this instinct developed the theme of the play, which was the unsettling effect that a muscular, stupid, but lovable lout had upon the lives of a group of women in whose presence he was placed for only one day.

The version of *Picnic* which Inge considers final was performed in Hyde Park in August, 1952, under the title *Summer Brave*. It is similar to the early version of *Picnic* which the author later changed considerably at the urging of Joshua Logan who directed the play which opened at the Music Box Theatre on February 19, 1953. This opening night was more traumatic than that of *Come Back, Little Sheba*, for Inge, who had established a reputation, was now putting it on the block. Joshua Logan's direction had not always pleased the author who on occasion left the theater in despair over what was being done to his play. However, Inge is quick to exonerate Logan from having purposely caused him any concern. He writes, "We had our ups and down with [*Picnic*], which I attribute mainly to my second-play nervousness and indecision. An unstable author, who isn't sure what he wants, is a great liability to a director; so if *Picnic* did not come off entirely to please me (as rumor had it), it was my own fault. Josh only sensed my indecision and tried to compensate for it."[20]

The public response to *Picnic* which played 477 performances before it closed on April 10, 1954, was gratifying, and the prizes which it won, amply attested to the warm approval with which most critics greeted the play. Even those critics who had adverse comment to make had to admit that *Picnic* was an example of competent craftsmanship. The movie rights were promptly bought on terms favorable to Inge and to his financial backers. However, Inge was still not entirely self-confident about his undeniably successful play. *Picnic*, after all, had been a reworking of material that he had written some time ago. He was still troubled by the nagging problem of creating new material, and this same difficulty has remained to the present time.

Inge's next play involved not only a reworking but a very great expansion of his one-act *People in the Wind* which he had written in 1953. *Bus Stop*, suggestive of Sherwood's *The Petrified Forest* or, in some respects, of Maugham's *Rain*, opened at the Music Box Theatre on March 2, 1955, under the highly sensitive direction of Harold Clurman whom Inge calls "the only real intellectual I know in the theatre."[21] *Time Magazine* called *Bus Stop* "the season's and possibly the author's best play."[22] Such critical statements were not unusual in the weeks following the play's opening. *Bus Stop* had a run comparable to that of *Picnic,* closing on April 21, 1956, after 478 performances. The film rights were sold, and a highly successful motion picture was made from the play.

Although the story line in *Bus Stop* was not strong, it served to provide the necessary mortar for the carefully studied, well-conceived character sketches of which the play is essentially composed.[23] Again in this play, both in its one-act version and in its extended version, the gallery of characters was drawn, more or less autonomously at first, and was then welded together into a single dramatic entity: first, by bringing them altogether in the microcosmic situation which the small restaurant provides; and, secondly, by presenting them at a time of crisis and decision. To say that *Bus Stop* is a reworking of old material is, in a sense, misleading; *People in the Wind* was the barest of sketches, a mere suggestion of fully realized drama; *Bus Stop* is a complicated revelation of human personality and group interaction.

As early as July, 1953, Inge had talked to an interviewer of reworking *Farther Off From Heaven.*[24] In the same interview he had indicated that he was also planning to do a one-act play about some rodeo cowboys in New York, which he thought might eventually be turned into a musical. Inge, who has been remarkably dependable in following his indicated plans, pursued them in this case just about as he had outlined them. His play about rodeo cowboys in New York was relocated, but *People in the Wind* and *Bus Stop* represented the fulfillment of the statement Inge had made two years in advance of the appearance of *Bus Stop* on Broadway. Now he turned to his earliest play, *Farther Off From Heaven,* and began a concentrated reworking working of it.

The result of Inge's efforts was *The Dark at the Top of the Stairs,* which opened on December 5, 1957, at the Music Box Theatre, directed by Elia Kazan. Actually, Inge had been working desultorily on this play for six years; but it was not until the winter of 1957 that the play was in its final form. It was written with a sure hand for, Inge states: "I was sure enough of my craft by the time I started writing *The Dark at the Top of the Stairs* to be able to take my craftsmanship more easily for granted."[25] Inge experimented technically in the play, and his experimentation was misunderstood by a number of critics who looked upon some of the play's greatest strengths as weaknesses. Nevertheless, there was little denying that the play was Inge's fourth hit in four tries. The Broadway reception was extremely cordial, and the film version was well received. When the play closed on January 17, 1959, after 468 performances, the critics could do little but marvel at the success of a man who wrote modest plays about the most prosaic of people, but who had never experienced a box office failure. And the clue to Inge's success appeared to be found in his characterization rather than in his dramatic structure. The playwright was suggestive, indeed, of Dickens in his realistic portrayal of everyday, commonplace human beings. But where Dickens often created his portraits by overelaboration, Inge underplayed his with the result that few of his characters emerge as caricatures.

The Dark at the Top of the Stairs marks the end of a significant phase of Inge's development both as playwright and person. From the sustained first phase of overwhelming artistic and commercial success extending from 1950 to 1959, Inge was now to pass into a difficult period of crisis from which he is still struggling to emerge.

IV *The Bubble Bursts*

William Inge had more faith in his fifth Broadway production, *A Loss of Roses,* than in most of his earlier productions. This faith was apparently not unfounded because Twentieth Century-Fox Studios paid $200,000 for the film rights before the play had been produced. Inge put half of his Twentieth Century-Fox money into the play and was virtually the sole backer of the production, the cost of which ran to some $125,000. Inge was convinced that this was his best play. It was an original script, not a reworking of something he had previously done. To Inge, it represented a logical step forward from *The Dark at the Top of the Stairs* in which the Oedipus problem, while elaborated upon, was not made the central concern, as in *A Loss of Roses.* The play went into rehearsal with Shirley Booth cast as Helen Baird. Miss Booth suggested numerous changes in the script; and Inge acceded to many of her wishes, although he began to fear that his play was growing weaker. Finally, feeling that her rôle was overshadowed by that of Carol Haney, who played Lila Green, Miss Booth withdrew from the cast after the Washington opening in October and was replaced in New Haven by Betty Field. Inge immediately realized that Miss Field was not strong in her rôle, partly because she had had so little time to rehearse. The author's artistic instincts told him to close the show, do considerable additional work on it, pursue a vigorous schedule of rehearsals, and open six weeks later after the Christmas holiday. However, the financial burden of this preparation and delay would have been staggering to Inge who already had much of his capital invested in the show; so, on November 28, 1959, *A Loss of Roses* opened at the Eugene O'Neill Theatre under the direction of Daniel Mann, who had earlier produced *Come Back, Little Sheba.* What Inge had nostalgically hoped would be an end-of-the-decade *Come Back, Little Sheba* developed into a total disaster, the effects of which were shattering to the author.

When the morning reviews appeared, Inge was incredulous—not that unfavorable things were being said about the play, but that the tone of some of the adverse reviews was so personally vengeful.[26] He had the feeling that he was being told he did not have the right to produce a play like *A Loss of Roses.* Inge, understandably shaken by the reception of the play, left New York unexpectedly in his convertible the day after the play opened and drove to Nashville in an attempt to sort out his emotional reactions about what had happened. *A Loss of Roses* closed on December 19, 1959, after only twenty-five performances. In time, as Inge began to evaluate the failure of *A Loss of Roses* in closer perspective, he tried writing a film play, *Splendor in the Grass.* Twentieth Century-Fox produced this film in 1961, and it won an Academy Award. Encouraged by the favorable reception which the film was accorded, Inge moved to Hollywood and did a second scenario, *All Fall Down,* which was entered in the Cannes Film Contest, and a third, *That Hill Girl.*

When Inge was interviewed upon moving to Hollywood, he was obviously suffering from a sense of sin such as that felt by Clifford Odets when he first left the Group Theatre and went to Hollywood in 1937. But Inge felt, in a sense, that he had been pushed from the nest; and he reacted by trying to convince himself that this was not so terrible: "I just have claustrophobia in New York. . . . I never liked New York. . . . I lose my feeling of identification there. It's too big. I was born and grew up with the natural world around me. I feel tense in New York. . . . New York is a hostile place."[27] In Hollywood, Inge tried to force the emergence of the new Inge. He judged a twist contest at the Peppermint Lounge West; he wrote for films, accepting the artistic compromise which this can imply; and he implied that he was writing essentially to make money. But Inge, fortunately, cannot bury the artist which surges within him. His crisis is not yet over; but there is every indication that its resolution is being reached on artistic grounds.

Inge's sense of futility after *A Loss of Roses* was reinforced by the adverse reception of his most recent play, *Natural Affection,* both on the road in 1962 and on Broadway early in 1963. However, it seems a hopeful sign that the author has moved back to New York where he is working on a novel and on a full-length play based on his one-act *Bus Riley's Back in Town.**

V *To Please Himself*

Inge once wrote that "a writer's first need is to please himself."[28] The implication of the statement and of Inge's entire article from which it is taken is that the author cannot consciously, panderingly write for his audiences. He goes on to clarify his initial statement by saying that a good writer will communicate to people something which has breadth and depth and vision, but he notes that "we resent . . . a playwright . . . who uses his medium as a means of persuasion. . . . A good play

* Since this book has gone to press, Inge has moved to Hollywood, presumably permanently. *Bus Riley's Back in Town* was produced as a film early in 1965, but at Inge's insistence, his name was expunged from the credits.

brings some illumination to life." Inge feels that a playwright should never ask his audiences to side with him. He assumes that audiences come to the theater "not to be told something but to find out something for themselves."

In an interview shortly after *Picnic* had brought Inge the Pulitzer Prize, he said: "A play should be admired for the experience it gives, not for the idea a playgoer comes away remembering. He should feel richer within himself, more responsive, more aware."[29] Such responsiveness and awareness were Inge's tie with his audiences in his early Broadway plays. The performances changed at least in some small way the lives of those who witnessed them and made them more responsive by making them aware of the necessity of love in its manifold aspects. And by far the most important love of which Inge writes in these plays, excepting possibly *Picnic,* is the love which represents the highest level of understanding and acceptance. Lola in *Come Back, Little Sheba* accepts Doc and loves him because she glimpses his frustration. In *Bus Stop,* Cherie accepts Bo's marriage proposal because he is awkwardly reaching out in loneliness and asking for someone to help him find realization. And in *The Dark at the Top of the Stairs* Inge exposes the horrifying effects brought about by lack of understanding—Sammy's suicide and the impasse which Morris and Lottie have reached in their marriage; and then, after bringing Cora and Rubin to the brink of just such an impasse, he ends the play with the blossoming of mature understanding between the two.

In reviewing all of Inge's plays, one can note dominant themes common to most of them. However, what Inge said in 1954 regarding his use of themes is still essentially true today: "I have never written a play that had any intended theme or that tried to propound any particular idea. . . . I want my plays only to provide the audience with an experience which they can enjoy (and people can enjoy themselves crying as much as laughing) and which shocks them with the unexpected in human nature, with the deep inner life that exists privately behind the life that is publicly presented."[30] Inge always begins his work with characters rather than with themes. Once he has sketched his people, he incorporates them into a situation from which theme emerges.

In an article which he wrote for the New York *Times* in 1955, Inge calls for more shows "that do not assume an attitude just to please, but that express something honest of life in their own original ways."[31] In the same article he warns that, although the dramatist has better reasons for his choice of profession than most people, inasmuch as his reasons exist in his very being, he must learn to grow beyond his work and not be possessive of it. However, after the trauma of *A Loss of Roses,* Inge reached out and drew his play protectively to him. He wrote in the Foreword to the Bantam edition: "After preparing a play for a New York opening, particularly if the play fails, it is very comforting for the author to get the manuscript back into his own hands and start getting it ready for his publisher. Then the author owns his script again, and he can clear from his mind all the confusing experiences he has had to cope with during production."[32] According to this same Foreword, he has adopted something of an existential stand that "man can only hope for an individual peace in the world."

A Loss of Roses is seriously out of focus; Lila Green should be the central figure in the play, but Inge has placed the emphasis elsewhere. Nevertheless, the play is generally very well conceived psychologically. The most serious objections to it have been to elements which could very easily be altered. *Natural Affection* is too heavily dependent upon the on-stage love-making encounters of the principals; the ending is also heavy-handed and would be much better hinted at rather than shown. But again, the play has distinct power which could be better channeled in a reworking of the material.

The significant literary gifts which characterized the Inge of the 1950's are by no means dead, nor even quiescent. *Splendor in the Grass* has great strength and attests to Inge's unusual ability to write with warmth and tenderness but with a psychological objectivity which is often downright clinical. Even the greatest literary Naturalists—Zola, Norris, Sinclair, Farrell—did not remain true to the Naturalistic credo of objectivity so faithfully as Inge has in his work.

One who views the period from 1959 to 1965 as the time of Inge's dramatic slump can take distinct encouragement from the fact that its products have had much more promise than the lesser ones of other significant dramatists. Certainly Odets' *Rocket to the Moon*, Sherwood's *Small War on Murray Hill*, Williams' *Battle of Angels* fail much more fundamentally than does any of Inge's major work.

CHAPTER 2

Success Is Counted Sweetest

> ". . . what can you do with
> the love you feel? Where is
> there you can take it?"
> —From *Picnic*

HAROLD CLURMAN comments in *Lies Like Truth*, that "the success racket consumes and wastes talent mercilessly" (14). Everyone knows what to do "if at first you don't succeed"; but a greater problem seems to be, for the writer at least, what to do if he does succeed. Once the success image is established, a writer is expected to maintain it, even though success often deprives him of the privacy which is necessary to productive creative talent.

The early recognition and success which *Come Back, Little Sheba* brought to William Inge left him first bewildered and then depressed. Inge had always looked forward to success; but, now that it was his, his emotions were not what he had expected they might be. In the Foreword to *4 Plays by William Inge*, he says, "Anticipating success (of any degree), I had always expected to feel hilarious, but I didn't. . . . I was in a funk. Where was the joy I had always imagined? Where were the gloating satisfactions I had always anticipated?"

Come Back, Little Sheba was followed by three plays—*Picnic, Bus Stop,* and *The Dark at the Top of the Stairs*—which were outstandingly successful commercially. It is in itself remarkable that Inge was able to compete successfully with his first Broadway production. Yet he wrote in 1958: "My plays since *Sheba* have been more successful, but none of them has brought me the kind of joy, the hilarity, I had craved as a boy, as a young man, living in Kansas and Missouri back in the thirties and forties. Strange and ironic. Once we find the fruits of success, the taste is nothing like what we had anticipated." Steinbeck comments forcefully upon the meaning of success in his short novel, *The Pearl,* in which Kino, the simple Indian pearl diver, finds "the pearl of the world." And what Kino learned so bitterly in *The Pearl,* Inge came to learn during the whirlwind decade of his greatest recognition: Success does not mean that the game has been won; it merely means that the stakes are higher and the competition fiercer.

The four plays dealt with in this chapter are very much concerned with the meaning of love in our society. But they are even more concerned with the questions of personal and spiritual isolation. The characters in these plays are cast in a given social milieu; but each is hindered in his attempt to find identity in his milieu by his great difficulty in communicating with others on any but a superficial level. More serious and pessimistic than even this situation, however, is the fact that so few of the characters really come to grips with themselves. Most of them are serving time toward an end which is unclear to them, living out days and weeks which involve only monotonous repetitions of commonplace human activities. At the end of each play, Inge suggests that a solution has been achieved—Lola and Doc in *Come Back, Little Sheba* have a reconciliation; Madge, in one version of *Picnic,* follows Hal, and in another version goes back to the life which she has been living; Cherie in *Bus Stop* consents to marry Bo and go off to Montana with him; Cora in *The Dark at the Top of the Stairs* follows Rubin upstairs with the implication that their marriage will now enter a more satisfactory stage. But in each case one is left with the nagging question of whether anything has really changed. Is the solution in each case not the result of a tremendous compromise, and is it not symptomatic of spiritual and emotional bankruptcy? Is Inge suggesting that the solution postulated will be a permanent one? And, if permanent, is this adjustment not, perhaps, the greatest defeat of all? Does this solution not represent an adjustment by default rather than by design?

In his first four Broadway productions, Inge presented life with intense realism. Willard Thorp has said, "The realism of his plots and dialogue suggests the kind of dramas with which the playwrights of the early 1920's broke the earlier tradition of sentimentality and melodrama in the theatre."[1] This undeniable realism stems largely from Inge's awareness that there is a great deal of fraud in human behavior. He is quoted as having said, "As a child, I was struck by the fact that the women there were always protesting, while men pursued. I got the idea that women hated men. I later came to the conclusion that this was an act— that there was a certain artificiality in their attitude. Some women love so passionately that they're embarrassed about it because it makes them dependent on men."[2] This statement is basic to an understanding of the man-woman relationships in Inge's plays; and in these relationships is found the key to his fundamental realism. He strips bare human motivation; and, like Williams, Miller, and McCullers, Inge brings one face-to-face with the compromises which man is forced to make in a society which is at best impassive and which may often be actively malevolent.

I Come Back, Little Sheba

Come Back, Little Sheba is generally considered Inge's best play.[3] In it Inge's primary concern is to present human motivations and behavior; however, the play, based on one of Inge's early short stories, has greater structural unity and a stronger story line than any of his other plays with the possible exception of his scenario, Splendor in the Grass. But most of what has been written about Come Back, Little Sheba has not noted the care with which Inge brought unity to his script.

Come Back, Little Sheba is largely a study of contrasts, a presentation of theses and antitheses. If there is any synthesis, it is found in the resignation with which the two major characters, Doc and Lola, face the prospect of continuing their lives together. They are not motivated by any very positive forces to face the fact of spending the remainder of their lives together. Lola has no choice. She has tried to escape from her situation by telephoning her mother and asking to come home. "Do you think Dad would let me come home for a while?" Lola asks her mother. Then her speech continues, "I'm awfully unhappy, Mom. Do you think . . . just till I made up my mind? . . . All right. No, I guess it wouldn't do any good for you to come here . . . I . . . I'll let you know what I decide to do" (100).* And Doc, having just re-turned from the "drunk tank" at the City Hospital, says to Lola: "Don't ever leave me. *Please* don't ever leave me. If you do, they'd have to keep me down at that place all the time" (115). Each has had his decision made for him. Lola has no place to go if she leaves Doc; she is thirty-eight years old, she is unattractive, she is untrained, and she has never worked. Doc looks to Lola as his only means of evading the terror of the drunk tank. They will stay together for the rest of their lives; but they will do so only because the alternatives are so hopeless.

Come Back, Little Sheba is a tale of personal failure and frustration, and of the attendant loneliness which is inevitable for the two central characters, Lola and Doc, who have been married for twenty years when the action of the play takes place. The garrulous Lola sketches in the past in reminiscences with Doc. She has been overly protected by a suspicious father who approved of none of her suitors until Doc, then a pre-medical student, appeared. The audience is told that Doc was a fine figure of a young man—the audience is asked to accept this fact on faith, for there is no real evidence within the play itself that Doc has ever been anything but mediocre—and that Lola was a beauty queen in high school. Doc was a shy suitor who courted Lola for a year before he dared to kiss her; and, when he finally did kiss her, the emotional pitch of the experience caused tears to well up in his eyes. But, having sufficiently overcome his basic reticence to kiss Lola, Doc proceeded with great dispatch to get her pregnant and then to marry her. The baby was lost, and Lola was left sterile, apparently because the delivery of the child was botched by a midwife to whom Lola went because she felt too guilty to go to a regular obstetrician.

Through Lola's garrulous ramblings to her roomer, Marie; to Marie's muscular lover, Turk; to the postman; the milkman; and the next door neighbor, the audience is told in considerable detail of Doc's alcoholism and of how he is overcoming it, of Doc's refusal to let Lola take a job in the early days of their

---

* All references are to the first edition of the play published by Random House in 1950.

marriage, of the reaction of Lola's father to her pregnancy, and of all manner of other data which provide a background for the play. Inge takes care of the necessary business of the play by using Lola as a one-woman chorus. While the device is contrived and tiresome, it covers the ground efficiently and in relatively little space. It also serves to highlight Lola's present frustration and loneliness—she will talk to anyone, but no one wants to listen—and to heighten the monotony of the early parts of the play to such an extent that the ultimate clash between Lola and Doc will, by contrast, have the effect of a tidal wave of action and of emotional intensity.

The slow build-up to the drunk scene in *Come Back, Little Sheba* has been considered by most critics to be a technical flaw. Most people who have written about the play have considered this scene to be surging with vitality, but they have been distressed that the action was so long in coming. However, Inge's design in delaying the crucial action was well calculated. He has said that he conceived the pace of the play to be like the pace of a tornado—frighteningly quiet, then unbelievably violent.[4] The drunk scene itself was seventeen minutes long in the New York staging of the play which Daniel Mann directed. Mann capitalized on the violence of this scene, and Sidney Blackmer was injured several times when he performed it. But Blackmer said that this climactic scene was "easier to play than the scenes of restraint and repression which lead up to it and which, by contrast, make the explosive scene so expressive."[5] This sudden action provides the most notable structural contrast in a play whose content is largely dependent upon the constant contrasts within it.

An overwhelming contrast within the play is that between Lola and her roomer, Marie, an art student with a very realistic outlook and with the morals of a cat. Lola, beautiful when she was Marie's age, is now overweight, sloppy, and shiftless. Marie is planning to marry her socially prominent, well-fixed suitor, Bruce; but Bruce lives in Cincinnati, some distance from where Marie now finds herself, so she carries on an affair with Turk, a wooden-headed hurler of the javelin. Indeed, the night before Bruce is to arrive for a visit, Turk stays in Marie's room. And, when Lola asks Marie if Turk won't feel badly about Bruce's coming, Marie says he'll be "sore for a little while, but he'll get over it. . . . He's had his eye on a pretty little Spanish girl in his history class for a long time. I like Turk, but he's not the marrying kind" (87).

The major pleasure in Lola's life now comes from her vicarious experiences through Marie. In Lola's stalwart approval of Turk and in her acceptance of Marie's affair with him are found, first, the basis for a significant cause of conflict between Lola and Doc; and, secondly, an indication that Lola, who was forced into marriage with her bashful suitor, has always hankered for the sheer animal pleasure which a brute like Turk could provide. Lola's last dream, which involves the throwing of the javelin, reinforces the basic phallic fascination which Turk holds for her. He, of course, holds the same sort of fascination for Marie, and there is no indication in the play that Bruce does; however, Bruce is the kind of boy that a girl marries. The implication is that, given twenty years of marriage to Bruce, Marie might well turn into a second Lola.

In the character of Turk, Inge is experimenting with the Stanley Kowalski type made classic by Williams in *Streetcar Named Desire*. The T-shirt is his emblem; he is long on bulging biceps and short on brains; he is best described as a male animal; and he flutters feminine pulses by his overwhelming sexuality. He is awkward in any place smaller than a stadium; he is gauche; and he is crude. He is destructive but commanding, and it is this quality which makes him irresistible. In the figure of the milkman, we see another sketch of the muscleman, but one less fully realized than Turk. However, Inge is to reach fruition in his portrayal of this type when he presents Hal in *Picnic* where the center of the action and the motivating force behind the action are dependent upon the sexually disturbing male.

Lola has been essentially a pure woman all her life. She now feels somewhat cheated at never having known any man other than Doc. But this feeling is something which she cannot acknowledge even to herself. She and Doc are separated from each other by years of faulty communication or of no communication at all. They do not know each other well enough even to be angry with one another. It is notable that they are always polite to each other in much the way that people are who have just met. Their aggressions are buried in indifference, in resignation, in apathy, except when Doc is drunk. There is no bickering, for example, when Doc corrects Lola. She has said, "You'd think after working so hard all day I'd be pooped." Doc responds, "Baby, don't use that word." She answers, "I'm sorry, Doc. I hear Marie and Turk say it all the time, and I thought it was kinda cute," but Doc tells her, "It . . . it sounds vulgar," and she responds, "I won't say it again, Daddy." (47-48). This is the sort of amiability which only apathy can produce. A further example of this avoidance of any unpleasantness—as well as an example of the lack of sensitivity which makes communication between Doc and Lola well nigh impossible—occurs when Lola has steamed open Bruce's telegram to Marie and read it. Doc chides Lola for this act: "Baby, nice people don't do things like that. Don't you understand? *Nice* people don't." But Lola does not understand. "I don't see any harm in it," she tells Doc. "I steamed it open and sealed it back. She'll never know the difference. I don't see any harm in that, Doc." And Doc just gives up, saying, "O.K., Baby, if you don't see any harm in it, I guess I can't explain it" (60-61). After twenty years together, Lola and Doc share virtually no common ground; and each retreats from the possibility of creating any.

Sharply in contrast to the slatternly Lola is her next-door neighbor, Mrs. Coffman. We are told early in the play that Mrs. Coffman doesn't have Lola's easy life: "When you got seven kids to look after, you got no time to sit around the house, Mrs. Delaney" (28). Just as the beautiful Marie reëmphasizes Lola's unattractiveness, the busy, family-centered Mrs. Coffman serves to show Lola as a lazy wastrel. And there is a further contrast in the fact that Lola is childless and barren, whereas the ample Mrs. Coffman has seven children. Just before Mrs. Coffman exits from her first appearance in the play, she tells Lola in annoyance and with some superiority that she cannot have coffee and chat with her because "I got work to do, Mrs. Delaney. I got work to do" (29). Then the milkman appears on the scene and says, " 'Morning, Mrs. Coffman," calling her by name; but, when Lola appears and says, "Hello there, Mr. Milkman. How are you today?" he replies, " 'Morning, Lady." This double rejection reinforces Inge's presentation of what Lola's life has generally been.

Her husband apparently rejects her as a wife. Her father rejects her because she became pregnant outside of wedlock. Turk and Marie put up with her, but Turk shows annoyance at her ubiquitousness, and Marie reacts out of pity rather than out of genuine fondness or respect.

Lola is totally at sea. She looks back upon twenty years of marriage which she really has nothing to show for. Her most noteworthy achievement has been in keeping Doc away from the bottle; but there is not a line in the play which would indicate that she has ever in her entire thirty-eight years experienced anything which might legitimately be called fulfillment. And partly because of this fact, she is too emotionally immature to have any stable relationship with another human being. She finds herself, as Auden writes, "Alone and afraid, in a world I never made"; and the double meaning of the last word applies fully to Lola. Inge implies in this and in much of his other work that loneliness and fear are part of the human condition and that the best man can hope for in life is the sort of compromise which Doc and Lola finally make to keep from being alone. Each has robbed the other of any chance for finding a satisfactory human relationship, and an almost hysterical fear becomes the single bond between them. Each is in the sort of trap which Eliot talks about in *The Cocktail Party*, where Edward and Lavinia, like Doc and Lola, simply resign themselves to trying to make the best of a hopeless situation.

The interesting dynamics of the relationship between Doc and Marie show Inge in highly satisfactory control of the situation with which he is working. Lola tells Doc, "If we'd had the baby she'd be a young girl now; then maybe you'd have *saved* your money, Doc, and she could be going to college—like Marie" (55). It is obvious that Marie is a surrogate daughter to both Doc and Lola. But she is more to each as well: to Lola, she is the means for vicarious fulfillment; but to Doc, she represents all that might have been. Doc, who is in love with Marie, is afraid to admit this feeling to himself; and, in his twisted emotional state regarding her, he becomes virtually obsessed by the illusion of her purity. To Turk, who represents the threat to this illusion, Doc reacts predictably with hatred. It is largely this hatred which precipitates the basic conflict between Doc and Lola. Doc is completely appalled because Lola encourages the Marie-Turk affair and because she even takes positive action to promote it by welcoming Turk to the house and by leaving Marie alone with him in the evening. But the one time that Doc rises above his apathy, without being stimulated by alcohol, occurs when he complains to Lola because she is permitting Turk to pose for Marie in his track suit. Lola explains that Marie is "just doing a picture of him" (44); but, as the curtain falls, Doc very angrily tells Lola: "All right, but if anything happens to the girl I'll never forgive you."

There can be no doubt that Inge intends Doc to be portrayed as loving Marie in more than a paternal way. Early in the play (15), he has Doc pick up Marie's scarf and look at it fondly; and this action recurs (77) when Doc picks up Marie's scarf and fondles it in Act II. Inge indicates the ethereal sort of love which Doc has for Marie when Doc turns on the radio and, according to the author's directions, "very unexpectedly he comes across a rendition of Shubert's famous 'Ave Maria,' sung in a high soprano voice. Probably he has encountered the piece before somewhere, but it is now making its first impression on him. Gradually he is transported into a world of ethereal beauty which he never knew existed. He listens intently" (47). Lola intrudes upon his reverie with a slam of the back door and an announcement that she is "pooped." The mood is shattered. And Inge returns to this idea; for, when Doc is holding Marie's scarf for the second time and the sound of Turk's laughter reaches him from Marie's bedroom, the directions say, "It sounds like the laughter of a sated Bacchus. Doc's body stiffens. It is a sickening fact that he must face and it has been revealed to him in its ugliest light. The lyrical grace, the spiritual ideal of Ave Maria is shattered" (77). Shortly after this episode Doc "gives in to temptation, grabs bottle off shelf, then starts wondering how to get past Lola with it" (83). The fondling of the scarf in the first act is followed by Doc's complaining to Lola about Turk and by the only display of anger we have from Doc in the play, except when he is drunk. And, predictably, the fondling of the scarf in the second act is followed by Turk's laughter, by Doc's yielding to temptation, and by the sequence of events which leads to the violent drunk scene.

Marie is unwittingly the triggering device in the play. She is never fully aware that Doc is jealous of Turk, even though Turk tells her: "He hates my guts. . . . If you ask me he's jealous. . . . I've always thought he had a crush on you" (66). But Doc never shows his jealousy or his disapproval of Turk when Marie is present. When Lola suggests that he speak to Marie if he objects to Turk's posing for her in abbreviated attire, Doc answers, "No, Baby. I couldn't do that" (41). And the stage direction just before Doc's statement indicates, "He'd never mention anything disapproving to Marie." But Marie has created the situation about which Doc and Lola now disagree, and this situation causes Doc to retreat again to the bottle. If there is any hope at the end of the play, it is in the fact that, when Doc returns home from City Hospital, Marie has left with Bruce to be married. Perhaps with Marie gone, Doc and Lola will achieve an even keel, but it is doubtful that they will ever find identity.

Doc, as one of the two central characters in the play, is never so fully realized dramatically as Lola. The audience is told what Doc might have been; indeed, Doc himself says, "If you can't forget the past, you stay in it and never get out. I might be a big M.D. today, instead of a chiropractor; we might have had a family to raise and be with us now; I might still have a lot of money if I'd used my head and invested it carefully instead of getting drunk every night" (56). But one wonders. Is it possible that Doc ever had the potential of being "a big M.D."? In the play there is no convincing evidence that he had. Of course, Inge might here be trying to indicate how utterly and completely Lola has drained him of every vestige of the potentiality which he had once possessed. But it is not entirely convincing that anyone so lacking in drive as Doc could have had much initiative to begin with. It seems more probable that Doc has found his level, that he has achieved his best, or very nearly so. Possibly he has clung to Lola because, either consciously or subconsciously, he realizes this fact; and he sees Lola as his rationalization both to himself and to the world. She stands as the visible evidence of the great sacrifice he has made.

The drunk scene provides a telling insight into what Doc really feels. It is a well-motivated scene, and the motivation—essentially Doc's unacknowledged love of Marie—is sustained throughout the crucial part of the play's climax. Doc pretends—both to Lola and to himself—that he is angry because Lola has cleaned the house and prepared a good meal not for him but for Marie's fiancé, Bruce. But the real reason for his wrath, of course, is that his desire for and jealousy of Marie are overpowering him. Even when he is drunk, he must repress this fact; but he reveals it obliquely, first, by saying, "You won't even sweep the floors, till some bozo comes along to make love to Marie" (96) and, secondly, by flourishing a hatchet and by railing, "I oughta hack off all that fat, and then wait for Marie and chop off those pretty ankles she's always dancing around on . . . then start lookin' for Turk and fix him too" (97). It is significant that Doc doesn't propose to kill Marie; he proposes to mutilate her, and in such a way that she will be unable ever to walk away from him. This desire to mutilate the loved one—whom he cannot have as she now is—is very sound psychologically. In a sense Doc is in the *Ethan Frome* situation; but in *Ethan Frome* mutilation occurs when death was intended, and the bitterness of Ethan's unrequited love is made the more poignant as Mattie Silver grows into a hag and comes to have a much sharper tongue than Zeena ever had. Doc's speech also implies not that he wants to kill Turk, but that he wishes to castrate him: the word "fix" clearly has such a connotation.

Doc's ideal of purity is very much tied up with his veneration of his mother, and this is one reason that he cannot face his own feelings toward Marie. There exist in him Oedipus problems, deeply subconscious, which make his feelings for Marie unbearable for him. When he pulls the cloth off the table and when the Haviland dishes, a wedding gift from his mother, go crashing to the floor, he shouts, "My mother didn't buy those dishes for whores to eat off of" (96).

One of the play's major contrasts is presented with great irony when Doc has been taken to the City Hospital. No sooner has he left than Marie and Bruce enter. Having been out all night, they know nothing of the events which Marie has unknowingly precipitated. The young couple comes "springing into the room," and Marie's first words are, "Congratulate me, Mrs. Delaney" (107). She then announces that she and Bruce are to be married and that she is going to quit school and go away with him at once. The timing here is perfect dramatically. Lola realizes how completely alone she will be, and she now telephones to her mother, only to suffer a rejection from her. Her isolation and loneliness at this point are complete. The sense of depression at the curtain of Act II, Scene 3, is total. It seems that all hope has been eclipsed, and from this desperate state Lola must begin to rebuild. The irony of Marie's first words when she returns indicates the total breakdown of communication between her and Lola. Marie has room only for her own happiness.

The symbolism in *Come Back, Little Sheba* is pervasive and often obvious. Much of the symbolism is included in the dreams which have been the subject of much adverse criticism by the reviewers of the play. It must be noted, however, that the dream parts of the play were read by several psychiatrists, before production, and that they had no significant quarrel with them on technical grounds. It must also be remembered that Inge has said, "Lola's dreams have a dramatic function and purpose, I believe, whether a scientific one or not."[6]

The first dream the audience is told about is a recurrent one concerning the loss of Lola's little dog, Sheba. In this dream, Sheba is the symbolic representation of Lola's youth, and the loss of the dog is synonymous with the passing of her youth. Lola dreams that she puts Sheba on a leash and takes her downtown: "All the people on the street turned around to admire her, and I felt so proud" (7); and Lola was much admired in her own youth because of her beauty. "Then we started to walk, and the blocks [years] started going by so fast that Little Sheba couldn't keep up with me. Suddenly, I looked around and Little Sheba was gone. Isn't that funny? I looked everywhere for her but I couldn't find her. And I stood there feeling sort of afraid." But Lola is unable to believe that the loss is permanent, for she asks Doc, "Do you suppose it means Little Sheba is going to come back?" And Doc utters his inner wish when he says, "Yah. Little Sheba should have stayed young forever. Some things [Lola] should never grow old" (8). And the irony of this statement is that, although Lola is growing old, she has never become mature.

In three separate instances Lola indicates that she feels a sense of great loss. The first instance occurs when she is talking about Sheba and Doc says, "She just disappeared. That's all we know," and Lola answers, "Just vanished one day . . . vanished into thin air" (9). Later on, when she is reminiscing with Doc about their courtship, he says, "Baby, you've got to forget those things. That was twenty years ago," and Lola responds, "I'll soon be forty. Those years have just vanished—vanished into thin air" (53). And, finally, when she is fixing the flowers on the table she is preparing for her dinner party honoring Bruce, she comments about the lilacs: "Aren't they pretty? And they smell so sweet. I think they're the nicest flower there is." Marie responds, "They don't last long," to which Lola replies, "No. Just a few days." Marie answers, "By the first of the week they'll all be gone," and Lola, for the third time in the play, says substantially the same thing: "Vanish . . . they'll vanish into thin air" (85). But this time she is somewhat gayer and, commenting that "we have them to spare *now*," she gives Marie one to put in her hair. In this action there is the suggestion that Lola is perhaps gaining some perspective.

A pervasive symbol that appears along with Sheba in Lola's final dream (117-18), is the symbol of the javelin.[7] Turk, whose sexuality is emphasized throughout the play, is in training for spring track. He tells Lola early in the play, "They got me throwing the javelin." Lola doesn't know what a javelin is, and Turk tells her, "It's a big, long lance. You hold it like this, erect—then you let it go and it goes singing through the air, and lands yards away, if you're any good at it, and sticks in the ground, quivering like an arrow" (22). The sexual connotations are entirely obvious; but, lest the audience have any doubt, Inge later reiterates the meaning of this symbol in preparation for the meaning he intends it to have in the final dream upon which the suggested outcome of Doc and Lola's problems depends. Turk propositions Marie, who coyly says, "Turk, you're in training." He replies with a double entendre: "What of it? I can throw that old javelin any old time, *any* old time. C'mon, Baby, we've got by with it before, haven't we?" (70).

In the closing minutes of the play, Doc says that he might take up hunting and get a bird dog which would, of course, replace Sheba. Then Lola says that she has had another dream "about everyone and everything." The dream has taken her back to a scene of her youth, her high school, where she and Marie are going to the Olympics. She makes a point of saying that there were thousands of people there and that Turk was out in the field throwing the javelin. It is clear that the fact that thousands were watching helps to assuage Lola's guilt feelings at having watched throughout the play Marie and Turk at various stages of their love-making, a perversity for which Doc has chided her.

The man in charge of the games is Lola's father. In the dream Turk kept changing into someone else all the time, clearly indicating Lola's desire for acceptance and love. But Lola's father finally disqualifies Turk, as he had disqualified all of Lola's would-be suitors; and Turk is replaced on the field by Doc. And then Lola's dream brings from deep in her subconscious the memory of what Doc once was to her: "You picked the javelin up real careful [Doc is not impetuous like Turk], like it was awful heavy. But you threw it, Daddy, clear, *clear* up into the sky. And it never came down again. Then it started to rain" (118). Then Lola misses Little Sheba. She searches in the crowd for her and "all of a sudden I saw Little Sheba . . . she was lying in the middle of the field . . . dead. . . . It made me cry. . . . It made me feel so bad, Doc. That sweet little puppy . . . her curly white [virginal] fur all smeared with mud [loss of innocence], and no one to stop and take care of her [parental rejection]" (118).

As the play closes, Lola gives some indication that she is ready to face life on more realistic terms than before. She has already made a start by filling out the dairy order slip rather than waiting for the milkman so that she can trap him into having a prolonged conversation. But now she tells Doc, "I don't think Little Sheba's ever coming back, Doc. I'm not going to call her any more" (119).

Inge calls *Come Back, Little Sheba* a "pathetic comedy." It is certainly not a tragedy in either the classical or modern sense of tragedy, primarily because the tragedy took place long before the play opened and what remains to happen is not tragic in comparison. If the hero has had a fall—Doc's not becoming a doctor—the audience is introduced to him long after it and at a point where he does not show the potential for being anything more than he is.

At best the play is melancholy rather than tragic. The sub-theme of continuance is strong—at one point Doc says, "We gotta keep on living, don't we? I can't stop just 'cause I made a few mistakes. I gotta keep going . . . somehow" (56)—and one is left with the feeling that Doc and Lola will go on now that Marie has gone out of their lives, perhaps the richer for what they have suffered, but more probably not much different from what they have always been.

At the time the play appeared, the critics were somewhat divided in their opinions of it.[8] Now that Inge has made his mark, *Come Back, Little Sheba* is generally well regarded. Perhaps what Inge said about the audience reception of a new play-wright, might also be said of the critical reception of a new play-wright: "It takes the slow-moving theatre audience one or two plays by a new author, who brings them something new from life outside the theatre, before they can feel sufficiently comfort-able with him to consider fairly what he has to say."[9]

II Picnic *and* Summer Brave[*]

Inge might well have had *Picnic* take place on May Day rather than on Labor Day; for in the New York production of the play, which Joshua Logan directed, the central figure, Hal Carter, the quintessence of sexuality, is, like the May Pole, a phallic repre-sentation about which a bevy of confused, dissatisfied, and frustrated women dance. However, the choice of Labor Day is also significant in that it heralds the end of summer which comes to represent in the play the passing of youth. The symbolic use of Labor Day is especially meaningful for Rosemary, the spinster school teacher who boards with the Owens family. This is her last day of summer before school starts, and also it is virtually her last chance to find a husband, for her youth is gone.

Rosemary feels more than a loathing at having to return to the dull repetition of another year of teaching, of "meetin' a bunch

[*]These two plays are treated together because they are different versions of the same play. Page references to *Picnic* (*Pic.*) will be to the version in *4 Plays by William Inge*. Page references to *Summer Brave* (*SB*) will be to *Summer Brave and Eleven Short Plays*. Both books are Random House publications.

of old maids for supper every night, then comin' back home alone" (*Pic.*, 130). She tells her fiancé, Howard, "Each year, I keep tellin' myself, is the last. Something'll happen. Then nothing ever does—except I get a little crazier all the time" (*Pic.*, 130). Every character in the play suffers from the same type of basic insecurity which makes Rosemary reach out pitifully toward Howard, not because she really loves him, but because she fears she will continue to live her life "till I'm ready for the grave and don't have anyone to take me there" (*Pic.*, 129).

Picnic, the basis for which was *Front Porch*, a fragmentary play written shortly after *Farther Off From Heaven*, consisted initially of little more than character sketches of five women living humdrum existences in a small Kansas town. Inge has written, "I was fascinated to find how . . . the women seemed to have created a world of their own, a world in which they seemed to be pretending men did not exist. It was a world that had to be destroyed, at least for dramatic values."[10] The microcosm in which Inge was originally working was a wholly feminine world. Into this world he introduced Hal Carter, and the entire play is concerned with the effects Hal's presence has upon the women.

As the play was originally conceived, there was no main character in it; and Inge was not eager at first to impose a story upon his sketches.[11] But, realizing that something had to happen to disturb his characters, he struck upon the fortuitous notion of introducing into the play a handsome, sexually disturbing young man. In Hal, Inge has created a composite figure who has the athletic ability and erotic appeal of Turk in *Come Back, Little Sheba*, but who also has the insecurity problems and the dependence of Doc in the same play. Inge gives Hal all the trappings indicative of virility—a dirty T-shirt, blue jeans, cowboy boots, and a great hairy chest which holds immense fascination for the women in the play, even though Flo and Rosemary heartily object to Hal's working around Helen Potts's yard without a shirt. But Inge also gives Hal all of the excuses he can for having an overpowering sense of inferiority and insecurity—he has spent a year in the reformatory because his mother did not care enough about him to save him from this fate when she had the opportunity; he has been rejected by his fraternity brothers because of his crudity; he has been forced to leave college for academic reasons; his father, with whom he had some rapport, has died after being jailed for public drunkenness; and his only friend, Alan Seymour, is basically not very fond of Hal.

In an unpublished master's thesis on Inge, Jerry L. Crawford notes that "the organizational core [of *Picnic*] is in the use of character. . . . The dramatic progression of *Picnic* is controlled by character through the beginning, middle, and end action." Crawford continues: "In all three organizational units Inge causes the spectator to be concerned primarily with the development of character, not with what is going to happen in the action."[12] In this respect, *Picnic* is significantly different from *Come Back, Little Sheba* in which the characterization, while still strong, is governed and directed both by the actions in which Marie and Turk engage and by the actions ensuing from Doc's drunkenness.

Picnic opens with immediate conflict in a minor key. Millie, the sixteen-year-old tomboy sister of the beautiful Madge, is sneaking a smoke on the back stoop. This act in itself indicates rebellion. The paperboy comes by and serves a double purpose dramatically. He antagonizes Millie and makes it obvious that she feels like the ugly duckling and that she resents her sister Madge because she is jealous of Madge's beauty which so eclipses her own physical assets that she has never attempted to appear feminine. The newsboy also prepares the audience for Madge's arrival on stage by commenting on Madge's unusual beauty. The rivalry and resentment between the two sisters is constant, for each is jealous of what the other has—Millie, of Madge's beauty; Madge, of Millie's intelligence.

Hal has already been introduced on stage when Madge makes her first appearance in the play. He has been seen working around Helen Potts's yard and has been described as a handsome vagabond. In an early exchange between Madge and the newsboy Bomber, it is revealed that because Madge is planning to marry Alan Seymour, the son of a well-to-do local banker, she cannot date other boys. Hal is brought into the action when he chivalrously comes to Madge's defense after Bomber has grabbed her arm. He sends Bomber scurrying, and he greets Madge, his face lighting up, with a simple "Hi." Madge responds with "Hi," and the two "stand looking at each other, awkward and self-conscious" (*Pic.*, 78). The animal magnetism between them is obvious in their meeting: and in this first five or six minutes of the action, the inevitable outcome is made entirely clear.

Hal and Madge have both been stumbling through life trying to find security. Hal has sought to find himself first by going to college on an athletic scholarship only to fail, and then by trying to break into films. His goals have always been unrealistic, but now he would like to settle down somewhere. Society has rejected him so often that he has very little self-confidence left, despite his displays of braggadocio. Madge, on the other hand, has found life much easier than Hal, or so it would seem. Beautiful, she appears to have much of the quiet confidence that beauty can give to a woman. Alan Seymour, an affluent young man, is worshipfully in love with her.

But Madge only appears to be secure. Her insecurities are soon revealed. She confesses to her mother that she does not feel comfortable with Alan's friends (*Pic.*, 81) because they have been to college and have traveled in Europe. Madge, who has not enjoyed these advantages, feels distinctly out of place when she is in the company of those who have. Madge also suffers from what might be called the "Marilyn Monroe problem"—she very much fears that *only* her beauty is appreciated; and she asks her mother, "Mom, what good is it to be pretty?" Then she says, "Maybe I get tired of being looked at. . . . It's no good just being pretty. It's no good" (*Pic.*, 84). Here, then, the audience comes to see Madge's double conflict; and this conflict is heightened throughout the first act by the fact that Alan's adoration of Madge is obviously based on his regarding her as a beautiful *object*, a showpiece of which he can be proud in public. It is also revealed that Alan's refinement is stronger than his virility. In a rather awkward scene between Flo and Madge, Flo asks if Alan ever wants to go beyond kissing when he is out with Madge. Madge, much embarrassed, admits that he does; then when Flo asks, "Does Alan get mad if you—won't?" Madge replies, "No. . . . Alan's not like *most* boys. He doesn't wanta do anything he'd be sorry for" (*Pic.*, 80). The Hal-Alan situation is, of course, broadly equatable to the Turk-Bruce situation in *Come Back, Little Sheba*.

The rising action in the first act of the play progresses in two separate lines of development, one for Hal and one for Madge. This rather heterodox dramatic procedure has caused some adverse criticism of the play's structure by critics who failed to realize what the author was trying to achieve by this method. Hal and Madge are both engaged in a conflict against society; and, as the two parts of the rising action progress, they become closer and closer together until they merge into a single line. Inge permitted the two developmental lines to remain merged in the Broadway production of *Picnic;* but, in *Summer Brave,* the lines separate in the falling action: Hal goes off to Tulsa; and Madge, having lost both Alan and Hal, goes back to her job in the five-and-ten. In both versions of the play, Hal has served the purpose of bringing Madge to a realization that she will never find fulfillment in life if she seeks only the grossly materialistic sort of security which her mother wants for her.

Madge's mother, Flo Owens, has an immediate, instinctive fear of Hal. She recognizes in him the same animal attractiveness to which she succumbed as a girl. Her life has been difficult and unhappy because she married a handsome, lovable, irresponsible stud who left her with two children and no forwarding address. Flo's first unpleasant encounter with Hal ends in her asking him to leave her property. It is, therefore, most ironic that she is finally forced by her admiration for Alan to accept Hal and to agree to have him come to the Labor Day picnic with them. When she discovers that Hal and Alan are old friends, she grudgingly says, "Any friend of Alan's is a friend of ours" (*Pic.,* 96); and Inge has effectively removed from the scene the major obstacle between Madge and Hal, a suspicious and objecting mother.

Helen Potts, the next door neighbor, to whom must certainly go the credit for discovering Hal, is an incurable romantic who insists upon calling herself "Mrs." even though her marriage to a young man was never consummated and was ended within days of its occurrence by an annulment which Helen's possessive, demanding mother obtained. Helen, whose young man was subsequently killed in the war, is now consumed by her clutching mother who is old and sick. Helen's only outward rebellion against the old woman is in her retaining the title "Mrs." Helen is a good soul; although she has ample cause to be bitter, she does not show any evidence of real bitterness. Rather, she is out-going and sincere. She grasps the opportunity to bring Hal into her house because Hal represents all that she has missed in life.

Mrs. Potts has no hope of attracting Hal herself, although she certainly would like to. Romantic though she is, Mrs. Potts is capable of facing and accepting the stark realities of life. This quality is especially evident when Madge and Hal start to dance together: "Then they dance slowly toward each other and Hal takes her in his arms. The dance has something of the nature of a primitive rite that would mate the two young people. The others watch rather silently." Mrs. Potts watches with fascination and then, indeed rather generously, remarks, "It's like they were *made* to dance together, isn't it?" (*Pic.*, 120).

Rosemary, the school teacher who also watches this dance, is already stimulated by an unaccustomed swig of whiskey she has had from Howard's bottle. But the inherent sexuality of the dance makes the awareness of frustration rise up unbearably in her. She needs a scapegoat; first she rails at Howard because he can't dance like that, then she throws herself at Hal in such an obvious manner that he, embarrassed, is forced to retreat—in essence, to reject Rosemary's advances. This action precipitates Rosemary's violent verbal assault upon Hal, and this unfair and uncalled-for attack arouses Madge's sympathy for Hal and leads ultimately to their having an affair.

Hal's presence on the scene is directly responsible for Rose-mary's compromising of Howard, a poor dupe who has little idea that an hour or two in the moonlight with Rosemary will result in his having to marry her. Rosemary is a fully realized and excellently portrayed character in *Picnic*. One might question the advisability of relegating her to a secondary plot in the play, for Rosemary seems sufficiently well realized to deserve a play of her own. Within *Picnic*, Rosemary and Millie are basically of the same fiber. Both affect a disinclination toward men be-cause both are afraid of rejection and are put on the defensive by their growing fear and insecurity. Millie finds sublimation in her reading and in her daydreams of becoming a novelist who will "shock people right out of their senses" (*Pic.*, 146). But for Rosemary no such sublimation is possible—despite all of her talk to the contrary, she is determined to claim her man. She spends hours working on her face and her hair; she dresses with great care. And in *Summer Brave*, Inge makes a point of having Flo say, "I think Rosemary'd smother in those winter clothes. I don't care *how* she denies it, she's out to get a man" (*SB*, 35).

Rosemary is fighting a far from unusual battle within herself. She has a sexual preoccupation, and this problem is compounded by her great fear of the future and by the restrictions imposed by the small town in which she teaches. Aging rapidly, she is more at sea even than Hal, despite her regular job and reasonably good income. Rosemary seems to have made a halfhearted adjustment to the grim realities of her life before Hal came on the scene. But she did so by attempting to make her personality more rigid; the result is that her personality structure is fragile, and the intrusion of Hal upon the scene is sufficient to shatter it. In *Summer Brave*, the audience is first introduced to Rosemary when she comes onto the porch, dressed in an old kimono with her hair in the process of being set and her face covered with cold cream. She says, "Shoot! I like a little town like this where you can go around as you please on a day off and nobody gives a darn" (*SB*, 18). But within a couple of lines she agrees with Flo that Helen Potts should make Hal put on his shirt when he is working around the yard.

Rosemary is probably going to be a better person for having yielded to her passion, thereby overcoming some of her repressions. Her passion, of course, is for Hal, but Howard is the best substitute she can find; so she leads him on and yields to him. The real clue to her salvation occurs, however, when Rosemary finally abandons the show of her much-touted independence and, in a disturbingly pitiful scene, begs Howard to marry her. In *Picnic* Howard goes off not saying whether he will accept Rosemary's proposal; and, as he exits, Rosemary, who is completely and totally humbled, cries to him, "Please, please." In this version of the play, Howard returns the next morning, probably to tell Rosemary that he will not marry her; but he does not get to see Rosemary alone because two other teachers are with her when he arrives. The implication is that Rosemary, before witnesses, traps him into saying he will marry her. However, in *Summer Brave*, Howard accepts Rosemary before he leaves but after she has humbled herself and begged him to marry her. In *Picnic* Inge allows Rosemary to retain at least a shred of dignity.

If anything in *Picnic* is out of focus, it is the secondary plot that gives formidable competition to the major plot and that is indeed strong enough to deserve full treatment itself. Rosemary remains one of Inge's most successful and convincing portrayals, and the fact that he presents her essentially as a comic figure only heightens the pathos of her situation. Rosemary, more than any figure in the play, drives home the theme that love requires humility.[13] She also sustains a theme which Inge presented in *Come Back, Little Sheba* and which carries through just as strongly into *Picnic*: What the world generally looks upon as love more often is the compromise which men and women make with each other to keep from being alone.

The rigidity of Rosemary's personality is not real; she has assumed the rigidity as a defense measure; however, she quickly abandons it in her desire to marry Howard. He claims that he is forty-two years old, that he has formed "certain ways of livin'," and that "it's too late to change." But Rosemary, who refuses to accept this statement, tells him, grabbing his arm, "Come back here, Howard. I'm no spring chicken either. Maybe I'm a little older than you think *I* am. I've formed my ways too. But they can be changed. They *gotta* be changed. It's no good livin' like this, in rented rooms" (*Pic.*, 129-30).

In *Picnic*, much more than in *Come Back, Little Sheba*, Inge is concerned with the pressures which society places upon its members to keep up appearances. Since the conflicts of the major characters are against society, it is reasonable that the author give some attention to the power exerted by society to bring these characters into conformity with community norms. Helen Potts, although she has little concern that people might gossip about her taking in a handsome young man, fears that people might come to look upon her as rejected. She sits down on Flo's porch, saying, "I *could* sit on my own porch, but I hate for the neighbors to see me there all alone" (*Pic.*, 88). She can stand all the frustrations of the dead-end existence which she dutifully leads; but she must give the impression of belonging. Howard is the figure in the play who is most sensitive to what people think and to what society demands. The examples of his sensitive reactions in this area are numerous. When Rosemary asks him why he cannot dance like Hal, he responds in *Summer Brave*, "Honey, if I danced that way, all my customers'd think I was unreliable" (69). And, in *Picnic*, when he has been inveigled into marrying Rosemary, he says, largely as a means of self-consolation, "A man's gotta settle down some time. . . . And folks'd rather do business with a married man!" (139). Howard faces the inevitable—what society decrees.

Millie, the only real iconoclast in the play, rebels against a society which worships the sort of beauty which Madge possesses. She states her feelings irrefutably when she tells her mother, "You're just saying I'm pretty because you're my mom. People we love are always pretty, but people who're pretty to begin with, everybody loves *them*" (*Pic.*, 104). Millie can rant about not wanting to marry, and she can affect the vocabulary of a stevedore; but, once Hal appears on the scene, it does not take her long to put on a pretty dress and to appear as feminine as possible. Her essential similarity to Rosemary is in her assumed attitude toward men. But Millie faces society defiantly and with some hope; Rosemary's iconoclasm, on the other hand, has been replaced by the fear and the insecurity which breed conformity.

While *Summer Brave* represents a strengthening of the Broadway version of *Picnic*, the ending of the Broadway play seems more satisfactory. Madge and Hal have a great deal in common—more certainly than Madge and Alan ever had—and it is altogether plausible that they might provide each other with some of the requisites of a satisfactory marriage. *Summer Brave*, on the other hand, is strengthened by the omission of the rather implausible story that Hal tells Alan of having been seduced and held up by two nymphomaniacal women who pick him up when he is hitchhiking—a tale that serves no real purpose in the play. The fact that Alan is a college graduate in *Summer Brave* rather than a student serves to broaden the cultural gap between him and Madge. Inge could have capitalized on the broadening of this gap most successfully if he had used it as a device for bringing Madge and Hal together in marriage; but, even as he uses it, much is gained, for in *Picnic* Madge and Alan will not be able to marry until Alan has completed his studies, and it is altogether possible that Alan will outgrow Madge in that time. But in *Sum-*

mer Brave, there is little standing in the way of their marriage.

Alan, despite the cultural differences between him and Madge, is convinced that he loves her. He has never been notably successful with girls; and, as Madge observes to her mother, he has an inferiority complex. He tells Madge: "At school, I didn't even *think* of the pretty girls. They were always so popular and there were always so many other fellows trying to get dates. I just kept my mind on my studies" (*SB*, 9). Alan is really incapable of meeting competition, and this speech early in the play is clearly the wink which Inge gives the audience to let it know what must indubitably happen.

In *Summer Brave*, Inge cuts the part about Hal's having spent the night in Alan's car; and, as a result, the part about Hal's running away from the police is evaded. Rather, Hal spends the night at Mrs. Potts's house, and the next morning Alan has a showdown with him and gives him money to leave town on the train. This departure would be more satisfying than that in *Picnic* had Inge retained those lines from *Picnic* in which Madge hears the train whistle and says: "Whenever I hear that train coming to town, I always get a little feeling of excitement—in here. . . . I always wonder, maybe some wonderful person is getting off here, just by accident, and he'll come into the dime store for something and see me behind the counter . . . and then decide I'm just the person they're looking for in Washington for an important job. . . . Or maybe he wants me for some great medical experiment that'll save the whole human race" (*Pic.*, 79-80). By scrapping these lines, he loses much of the impact of Hal's departure which might ironically have come to represent Madge's dream in reverse. It is important to notice in both plays that, although Madge is to marry Alan, she talks of escape—in *Summer Brave*, she talks of going off to New York or Chicago to be a model or an actress (12); and in both plays this talk of escape makes more plausible Madge's affair with Hal.

If Inge's first play had established his reputation in the theater, *Picnic* assured the skeptics that *Come Back, Little Sheba* had not been just a unique stroke of good fortune. The widespread recognition which *Picnic* received by winning three major drama awards caused Inge to be favorably compared to Williams and Miller.[14]

III   People in the Wind *and* Bus Stop*

One of Steinbeck's less successful, little-known works is entitled *The Wayward Bus*. Whether he had in mind Sebastian Brant's fifteenth-century rambling poem *Das Narrenshyff* when he undertook this work is not known; however, Steinbeck uses his bus much as Brant used his ship: he created a veritable Noah's ark on wheels whose cargo consisted of as many basic types of human being as the author could cram into it. It is doubtful that Inge had *The Wayward Bus* in mind when he wrote *People in the Wind* in the early 1950's; but, if he had had it in mind, one might certainly conclude that he did well to unload the bus on that stormy March night at a corner restaurant in a small country town between Kansas City and Wichita. The romantic comedy which in *Bus Stop*—an expanded version of *People in the Wind*—develops during the night when four bedraggled passengers, a bus driver, the local sheriff, and two waitresses, sit out a raging blizzard in the restaurant, might well be subtitled *The Anatomy of Love*. In this play, which Inge says he meant "only as a composite picture of varying kinds of love, ranging from the innocent to the depraved,"[15] the author once again pursues his recurrent theme that humility is the *sine qua non* of love, and this idea is here presented in both its positive and negative manifestations.

In *Come Back, Little Sheba*, the center of the stage was shared by Doc and Lola, and Lola emerged for most people as a central character with Doc running a close second. For most of the audience of *Picnic*, Hal Carter was a central figure whose hold on this position was quite tenuous; at times Madge or Rosemary or the entire gallery of women collectively threatened to emerge as central. In *Bus Stop*, Inge appears to have achieved the effect which he was irresistibly and progressively moving toward in his two earlier Broadway productions. *Bus Stop* does not have a single major character. Much of the play revolves around the

*All references to *People in the Wind* (PW) will be to the version which appears in *Summer Brave and Eleven Short Plays*; references to *Bus Stop* (Bus) will be to the first edition of the play, published by Random House in 1955.

pursuit of Cherie, the sexy, ungrammatical little *chanteuse* (she pronounces it "chantoosie") from the Kansas City stockyards, by the crude but ingenuous Bo Decker, a young rancher from Montana who insists upon marrying the stubbornly unwilling little sexpot because he has "been familiar" with her. One has the faintly amused feeling throughout the play that in this satirical presentation of conventional morality in reverse, Bo is pressing, with righteous indignation, toward the shotgun wedding which will make him an honest man. The pervasiveness of this feeling gives the play a sustained humor which probably acounts for a great deal of its popularity with audiences both on Broadway and throughout the country when it was made into a film starring Marilyn Monroe.

But, as important as Cherie and Bo are to the play, each of the other characters carries his full share of the burden in the development of Inge's exploration into the meaning of love. John Gassner labels all the characters, aside from Cheric and Bo, as "secondary"; however, viewing them in the light of their roles in the development of the theme of the play, one must more nearly describe them as equivalent characters. The only exception to this statement is found in the portrayal of the sheriff, Will Masters, who is a utility character. Gassner speculates that "some day, if left alone by producers, William Inge is going to write a play made up entirely of minor characters and come up with a major masterpiece."[16] This he has essentially done in *Bus Stop*, but one would necessarily stop short of calling the play a masterpiece.

If *Bus Stop* is basically an anatomy of love, albeit a very limited one, *People in the Wind* is an anatomy of loneliness. Inge's change in emphasis, as he began to rework his original material, is quite evident on even a casual reading of the two plays. *People in the Wind* is set exactly as *Bus Stop* is; however, the author gives himself less time to develop the situation in the earlier play. The bus arrives during a storm, but it is not detained by the storm. Therefore, what was to become a five-hour encounter in *Bus Stop* was a twenty- or thirty-minute encounter in the one-act play. Consequently, the overall relationships are dealt with in a most attenuated way, and the Bo-Cherie situation—Bo and Cherie are called just "Girl" and "Man" in *People in the Wind*—receives the bulk of the author's attention. Dr. Lyman—called merely "The Drunk"—is pictured only as a lonely man adrift. Presumably he has been rejected by the girl he wanted to marry, has found so much solace in alcohol that he has become too unreliable to hold his teaching position, and is now spending most of his life on buses between towns. The bus driver is essentially a stock character in the earlier play, and Grace is more hard-boiled than in *Bus Stop*. Elma Duckworth is cast as the wide-eyed innocent to whom are revealed details necessary to the development of the plot. Will Masters does not appear in *People in the Wind*, nor does Virgil Blessing.

However, the play has two characters who are not brought over into *Bus Stop* and this is the major clue to the shift in emphasis. These characters are identified as "Old Lady 1" and "Old Lady 2." They presumably are two unmarried women—they appear to be sisters, although their relationship to one another is never actually stated—who are going to visit Melinda who apparently is their niece. They are poor—"Can we afford a taxi?" (*PW*, 138)—and they are not entirely sure how warm a welcome they will receive when they reach their destination: "Maybe if we help with the work around the house, we can make things easier for Melinda and not get in the way" (*PW*, 146). These two women, one of them drinking bicarbonate to settle her nervous stomach, represent what happens in old age to those who have not formed close ties. They loom as one of two horrible examples to Cherie and Bo; the drunk is the other: "I've always been a very proud man. After all, a man *should* be proud, don't you agree. I loved her very much but I wasn't going to let her know she hurt me. If she didn't have the wisdom and the up-bringing to realize my own innate superiority to other suitors, then who was I to humiliate and degrade myself by telling her how very much I cared?" (*PW*, 142). And the result of the professor's pride is clearly seen at the end of the play where he laments, "I'll spend the rest of my life riding on busses" (*PW*, 146).

Grace's crassness and cynicism in *People in the Wind* are manifestations of her loneliness. People pass through her restaurant, but she has no permanent ties with anyone and is portrayed as someone in whom tenderness and warmth have been

replaced by the defensive mechanisms which she has con-
structed to protect herself from being hurt. Elma, as she appears
in *People in the Wind*, is involved in no romantic complications
and is a purely utilitarian character. She has just been graduated
from high school in the earlier play, and there is no indication
that she intends to continue her education. In *Bus Stop*, in order
to involve her in the love complication with Dr. Lyman, Inge
makes her still a high school student, a girl who is just coming
into an awareness of the meaning of love. She is a bright girl,
suggestive of Millie in *Picnic*. She, like Millie, is looking forward
to going to college; her unpopularity with boys is made evident
early in the play when Grace tells her, "Maybe you'd have more
boy friends if you didn't make such good grades. Boys feel kind
of embarrassed if they feel a girl is smarter than they are" (*Bus*,
8). Like Millie, she would "like to write a book about the
people [she] sees" (*PW*, 147).

The Bo-Cherie relation in *People in the Wind* is much less
convincing than in *Bus Stop*. In the former, Cherie tells Bo, "I
don't know you. You just came in the bus and sat beside me and
took my hand. I never saw you before in my life" (*PW*, 144).
And Cherie quails at the thought of going with Bo to his
Montana ranch only because he has not mentioned marriage.
When he tells her, "We'll be married. What kinda guy you think
I am?" (*PW*, 145), Cherie takes very little time to decide to
follow him back into the bus. Furthermore, in the early play,
Inge indicates that Cherie is on the bus because she is heading
for Hollywood to have a screen test. He lets the audience decide
the veracity of Cherie's statement to this effect. However, in
Bus Stop, Cherie has left her job in the Blue Dragon and has no
immediate plans. She makes vague references to going back to
Kansas City to work in a drug store. Inge also makes it apparent
in *Bus Stop* that Cherie has very little money: she does not order
two doughnuts until she has found out how much they cost. And,
when Elma tells Cherie that there is a little hotel down the
street where she might spend the night and escape from Bo, she
answers, "What ya take me for? A millionaire?" (*Bus*, 14). In
People in the Wind, however, Grace says to her, "There's a
little hotel across the way, but they'd have to get outa bed to let
you in," and Cherie replies, "I don't want to be any trouble"

(*PW*, 133). Inge also provides some background for the Bo-Cherie relationship in *Bus Stop* by having Bo first meet Cherie in the Blue Dragon where she completely captivated him by her rendition of *That Old Black Magic*. The ensuing friendship led directly to the bedroom—a new experience for Bo—and his claim upon Cherie is based upon his affair with her.

Bo is rough and crude in *People in the Wind*, and these qualities are explained by the fact that he, a rancher from Montana, is quite unused to the cosmopolitan sophistication to which Cherie has been exposed in Kansas City. In *Bus Stop*, he is still rough and crude, but the audience comes to know him better; moreover, the creation of Virgil Blessing aids greatly in Bo's characterization as a more lovable person. Virgil serves the dual purpose of providing the audience with background about Bo and of illustrating one of the forms of love with which Inge deals in the play—the form of love which the Greeks would refer to as *agathe*: love based upon charity rather than on eroticism. The name Virgil Blessing is in itself suggestive of the purity which is implicit in his devotion to the twenty-one-year-old Bo whom he has looked after for the past eleven years. And his name is especially significant at the end of the play when Virgil declines to return to Montana with Bo and Cherie but gives their marriage his blessing.[17]

Virgil stands in almost direct opposition to Dr. Lyman in *Bus Stop*. Dr. Lyman's tragedy is that "I never had the generosity to love, to give my own most private self to another, for I was *weak*. I thought the gift would somehow lessen *me*. *Me!*" (*Bus*, 108). Dr. Lyman, who is completely self-centered and realizes it, is apparently unable to change. Inge reinforces Dr. Lyman's self-centeredness by small touches such as that found in the direction immediately prior to the beginning of his performance of the Balcony Scene from *Romeo and Juliet* with Elma. The direction reads, in part, "He is a thoroughly selfish performer, too, who reads all his speeches as though they were grand soliloquies, regarding his Juliet as a prop" (*Bus*, 98).

Dr. Lyman's obvious nympholepsy also implies a deeply rooted self-centeredness. On the other hand, Virgil is the soul of genuine, unostentatious sacrifice. His devotion to Bo is so genuine that he has passed up the opportunity to have a home and family of his own; but, now that Bo has found the woman he wishes to marry, Virgil steps out of his life with rather touching grace. As the play ends, Grace has to close the restaurant; it is five o'clock in the morning and the bus has left. Virgil has nowhere to go, and Grace tells him, "Then I'm sorry, Mister, but you're just left out in the cold," to which the pathetic Virgil replies, as the curtain is rung down, "Well . . . that's what happens to some people" (*Bus*, 154).

In *Bus Stop*, Grace is much warmer and sweeter than she was in *People in the Wind*. Her attitude toward Elma—who, it must be remembered, is younger in *Bus Stop* than in the earlier play—is much more maternal. Indeed, one might be led to think that Grace is to Elma as Virgil is to Bo. It would seem an obvious solution for all concerned to have Virgil invited to the warmth of Grace's apartment—as Carl, the bus driver, had been earlier in the action; there each might have found the means of escaping the loneliness which seems inevitable. However, Inge moderates the happy ending of his romantic comedy with a sardonic twist. The only person in the play who represents purity, with the possible exception of Elma, is left out in the cold, completely alone. This situation, of course, supports the theme with which Inge is working—life without love is lonely; and Virgil has turned his back on love: "A long time ago, I gave up romancin' and decided I was just gonna take bein' lonesome for granted" (*Bus*, 70).

Dr. Lyman attempts to rationalize his loneliness, to imply that in it is his freedom; but, the more he drinks, the further his inhibitions slip and it is soon apparent that he is the most desperate character in the play. The author builds an aura of mystery about him by making it clear that he has an extreme concern with crossing the state line (*Bus*, 19-20). Later, Carl and Will have a whispered conversation about him, and the situation is finally spelled out with no uncertainty when Dr. Lyman tries to arrange a meeting in Topeka with Elma but urges her not to tell anyone. In *People in the Wind*, Dr. Lyman's nympholepsy is not brought to the fore; however, Inge reveals another facet of his personality which is not shown as such in *Bus Stop*. Dr. Lyman's retreat from a reality which is painful to him is partially manifested in his excessive drinking; but how total this desire to retreat is becomes apparent toward the end of *People in the Wind* when the following speech clearly represents his subconscious desire to return to the womb: "Hear the wind lashing at the houses? But inside that big warm bus, you don't feel it. You're warm and snug, cuddled up in your seat, and you can coast along through the night, sleeping like a baby. With no destination" (*PW*, 146).

A number of critics have objected to the emphasis on sex in *Bus Stop*. Theophilus Lewis calls the play a "Decameron-type story of the Kansas plains,"[18] and Eric Bentley concurred in feeling that the author might have toned down the sexual approach to his material.[19] Richard Watts, however, made the significant point that Inge is not writing about sex as a cheap, crass thing; he is using it to highlight the loneliness which man feels, the groping which man does to find love and understanding.[20] The casual affair which takes place between Grace and Carl emphasizes the loneliness which someone like Grace cannot escape. Toward the end of the play, Grace tells Elma, who now knows that Grace has had an affair with Carl, "I'm a restless sort of woman, and every once in a while, I gotta have me a man, just to keep m'self from gettin' grouchy" (*Bus*, 151).

Inge convincingly prepares the audience for the Grace-Carl part of the play which is used effectively to heighten the sense of lonely futility which Grace feels. One knows that Grace has some reason for asking Elma to let her get Carl's meal. A subtle implication by the author has been overlooked by many who have seen the play; for, in an early speech, Grace says: "Sometimes, at night, after I empty the garbage and lock the doors and turn out the lights, I get kind of a sick feelin', 'cause I sure don't look forward to walkin' up those stairs and lettin' myself into an empty apartment" (*Bus*, 6). At the very end of the play, the directions indicate that Grace "carries a can of garbage out the rear door . . . comes back in, locks back door, snaps wall switch, then yawns and stretches, then sees that the front door is locked" (*Bus*, 154). Virgil at this point has no place to go, but Grace has been satisfied for the evening. The portent of what happens here is that her life will remain empty; for, even though she is capable of kindness, she is not capable of sharing her identity with anyone else.

There is very little action in *Bus Stop;* the play is essentially developed through talk which Gerald Weales calls "the clumsiest exposition in the early Inge plays." He complains that "Elma Duckworth . . . wanders from character to character, gathering information as though she were a researcher for *Current Biography*."[21] This statement is demonstrably true; but the question remains of whether or not this weakness is very significant. The device of using one central character in this way is not unusual—note, for example, Gabby in *The Petrified Forest*—and, in a play which is more dependent upon thought than action, the method does not have a weakening effect. The revelation of pertinent material to Elma is handled gracefully, and one never has any strong feeling that this contrivance which is used to handle some of the necessary business of the play is forced or unconvincing. Inge protects against this impression by portraying Elma as a sincere, innocent sort of creature who enjoys talking and is easy to talk with—the audience sees this in the scenes involving Grace and Elma alone before the bus arrives.

Inge is also careful to prepare for the delay which will force the passengers on the bus and the driver to remain in the restaurant for several hours. Grace is careful to state that the bus will get to the restaurant: "The roads are OK as far as here" (*Bus*, 4). Then Will Masters comes in and makes clear that the bus will not get beyond the restaurant—"You're gonna have to hold 'em here, don't know how long. The highway's blocked 'tween here and Topeka. May be all night gettin' it cleared" (*Bus*, 9). Inge also prepares for the fact that there are only four passengers on the bus when one might have expected considerably more. Elma, as she looks out the window at the raging storm, says to Grace, "I bet the bus doesn't *have* many passengers. . . . I shouldn't think anyone would take a trip tonight unless he absolutely had to" (*Bus*, 5). It was structurally necessary for Inge to establish this point early, for he could not have handled his situation well had he brought too many people into the restaurant. It would have been impossible to focus attention as he did; and, had there been more customers to serve, it would have been impossible for Grace to make her exit and to have her affair with Carl.

Bo—a refreshing character who is completely undisciplined

and is motivated almost solely by his impulses—is announced to the audience by Cherie before he appears on stage. She tells how "he *put* me on the bus. I'm bein' abducted" (*Bus*, 15). Her story is not totally convincing because her abductor is, according to Cherie's own testimony, now asleep on the bus. Both in *Bus Stop* and in *People in the Wind*, Inge is also careful to prepare the audience psychologically for Cherie's eventual acceptance of Bo. In the one-act play, he clearly states that Cherie was not entirely cold to Bo's initial advances: "I'm not gonna forget . . . back there on the bus . . . before you got mad . . . how you kissed me . . . sweet and soft" (*PW*, 143). And in *Bus Stop*, Cherie does not deny her intimacy with Bo; she merely seems shocked that he should have taken seriously such a casual affair.

A large part of the play's humor is quite broad and results from Bo's innocence and provinciality. Bo fully expects Cherie to marry him when he tells her that he loves her. The dialogue here is amusing, but it is also quite touching since Bo has never considered the possibility that he might love someone who did not reciprocate his love:

BO: See there? I told her I loved her and I wanta marry her. And with a world full of crazy people goin' 'round killin' each other, *you* ain't got nothin' better t'do than stand here tryin' to keep me from it.

WILL: Yor overlookin' jest one thing, cowboy.

BO: Yor so smart. Tell me what I'm overlookin'.

WILL: Yor overlookin' the simple but important fack that the little lady don't love *you*.

(*Bus*, 53)

Bo, dumbfounded by this suggestion, responds comically with, "That polecat bastard! He said she din love me."

Bo is never presented as a wholly sympathetic character until well into the second act. Here Inge gives him a speech which makes him as sympathetic as Doc in *Come Back, Little Sheba* when he comes home from the City Hospital and begs Lola's forgiveness. Bo tells Virgil, "I hate to sound like some pitiable weaklin' of a man, but there's been times the last few months, I been so lonesome, I . . . I jest didn't know what t'do with m'self" (*Bus*, 69). Finally, Bo begins to realize that it is possible for a girl not to like him, and he begins to make an evaluation of himself. In a series of speeches which would lend themselves beautifully to musical comedy but which are also rollicking as straight drama, Virgil tries tactfully to indicate to Bo that he *might* succeed better with girls if he were just a bit more gallant. Bo is amazed at this suggestion and protests, "Gall—? Gallant? I'm as gallant as I know how to be" (*Bus*, 76). He then muses, "But a gal *oughta* like me. I kin read and write, I'm kinda tidy, and I got good manners, don't I?" Virgil, always attempting to be honest but kind as well, can only answer evasively, "I'm no judge, Bo. I'm used to ya" (*Bus*, 77). The good-natured banter in this scene is irresistible; the pace and timing are superb; and, under Harold Clurman's brilliant direction, the humor was exploited to the utmost.

Although Inge is not essentially concerned with the Bo-Cherie love conflict, he makes it apparent early in the play that Cherie is attracted by Bo and that she will not long resist his adoration. When she takes part in the mock nightclub perform-ance which Elma instigates, she sings the song which brought Bo to such ecstatic rapture in Kansas City. Obviously she is contriving to use *That Old Black Magic* to cast her spell on him again; and he reacts with all of the vigor which the audience has been told he displayed at the Blue Dragon. Also, Cherie seems to have a lacklustre future before her: "after a while I'll prob'ly marry some guy, whether I think I love him or not. Who'm I to keep insistin' I should fall in love. You hear all about love when yor a kid and jest take it for granted that such a thing really exists. Maybe ya have to find out fer yorself it don't" (*Bus*, 81). This speech is the clincher because the audience knows (1) that Cherie finds Bo attractive; (2) that she is adrift; (3) that Bo owns a ranch and is something of a solid citizen; and (4) that Bo has six thousand dollars in the bank. Unless all signs fail in fair weather, Cherie has to marry Bo. He is an excellent catch for someone in her position.

One might reasonably ask why Inge makes this fact so clear in the middle of the play. Does this not reduce the suspense and weaken the dramatic structure? It would if Inge were primarily concerned with the Bo-Cherie pursuit; however, he merely uses this conflict as a vehicle for writing more broadly about the question of love, and his concern in the remainder of the play is with the broader question. John Gassner is probably correct in his opinion that the Bo-Cherie conflict "paid reduced dividends as it went along."[22] The humor of the situation helped to sustain audience interest and reaction in the latter half of the play, but the central love conflict in the play might have been better handled in less detail.

The resolution of the central love conflict in the play comes only after the man, Bo, has humbled himself. Will Masters has had to restrain him and has now brought him back to the restaurant where he must apologize to everyone. Bo finds it especially difficult to apologize to Cherie, but he finally succeeds in doing so after Will tells him, completely in the Inge tradition, "A man don't deserve the things he loves, unless he kin be a little humble about gettin' 'em. . . . Being' humble ain't the same thing as bein' *wretched*" (*Bus*, 119-20). Bo apologizes and then, as Robert Brustein puts it, "indicates his tamed domesticity by solicitously putting his leather jacket around her [Cherie's] shoulders."[23] Bo, through humility, proves his point—"A man's gotta right to the things he loves" (*Bus*, 119). Hal made essentially the same point in *Summer Brave*—"I'm a poor bastard, baby. A guy's gotta *claim* the things in life that're *his*" (98). Bo and Hal are both motivated by the same sort of impetuosity and are both reaching out hungrily for the love which can vitalize and give meaning to their lives.

Bus Stop is dramatically a tight play. The time span of five hours during which the entire action occurs imposes upon the author the task of filling in a great deal of background material; Elma Duckworth and Will Masters are used to draw necessary information from the other principals in the cast. The physical confinement of the restaurant also aids in bringing dramatic unity to the play. Despite its confinement, the restaurant is a place out in the open compared to the bus, and this element is emphasized by the illumination of the set: ". . . illumination comes from two badly shaded light bulbs that hang on dangling cords from the ceiling" (*Bus*, p. 3). *Time Magazine* referred to Inge's bus as a symbol of "his whole lost, seeking, itinerant world."[24] Certainly the bus carries a major portion of the play's symbolic weight. However, it must also be remembered that the bus represents as well as privacy (for Bo and Cherie), a means of escape (Dr. Lyman), and security from a hostile world (Dr. Lyman).

The hope which *Bus Stop* offers is certainly more convincing than that offered by *Come Back, Little Sheba* which ends merely in a rather unhappy and unsatisfying compromise in which Doc and Lola will suffer quietly for the rest of their days. However, Bo and Cherie have come to satisfactory terms; and it is highly probable that the basic physical attraction which they first found in each other will blossom into the sort of balanced love which is the chief ingredient of a happy marriage. Bo is lovable and touchingly genuine; Cherie is appreciative of him as the play ends. Moreover, she is much in need of someone who will love her, for she has never known what it is to feel really wanted.

Inge suggests at the end of the play that Dr. Lyman, too, has benefited significantly from the bus stop. He tells Elma, "Dear girl, let us give up our little spree, shall we? You don't want to go traipsing over the streets of the State's capital with an old reprobate like me." Elma answers, "Whatever you say," and then Dr. Lyman muses, more to himself than to Elma, "Ah! sometimes it is so gratifying to feel that one is doing the 'right' thing, I wonder that I don't choose to always" (*Bus*, 137). These lines, while they do not convince one that Dr. Lyman is now a reformed character, do indicate that he is a man of some conscience; and, long dormant, it has apparently been reactivated by the events of the evening.

The play's most hopeful line comes at the point where Bo, shocked at the revelation of Cherie's past, reconsiders his desire to marry her. But then he says that Virgil "thinks I'm virgin enough fer the two of us." Then he adds, "and I like ya like ya are, Cherry. So I don't care how ya got that way" (*Bus*, 142). Bo's willingness to accept Cherie is now based upon such a realistic outlook that one is left with the feeling that their marriage has every chance of success.

Henry Hewes summed up *Bus Stop* accurately when he wrote that Inge seems not to have done "much more than interweave a trio of not very startling sketches. . . . they all deal with the conflict between security produced by selfishness and true love." Mr. Hewes continues: "The play's chief distinction lies in the way Mr. Inge has served up banal characters with their most sentimental fat trimmed off."[25] The emotions portrayed in *Bus Stop* are, in the final analysis, stark and undramatized. Herein is found the greatest strength of Inge's extreme realism. His clinical objectivity increased steadily from *Come Back, Little Sheba* to *The Dark at the Top of the Stairs,* and it was increasingly reinforced by his unadorned use of language and by the classic starkness of his settings.

It becomes increasingly evident in the work of Inge that love is to be discovered through sex and that problems are more often to be solved in bed than in the parlor. Inge is aware most fully of what Brooks Atkinson calls "the illusiveness of human experience."[26] His characters often seek to overcome this illusiveness and to escape from their loneliness through sex. The most promising indication that Inge can offer regarding the possibility is personified in the awkward, innocent Bo; his affair with Cherie was little different from Carl's affair with Grace except for the fact that in Bo, love and passion merged into a single line which was eventually to touch Cherie so that she could for the first time in her sordid existence look forward to a total, balanced relationship with a man.[27]

IV   The Dark at the Top of the Stairs*

The Dark at the Top of the Stairs has been referred to as a patchwork. Herein lies much of the critical misunderstanding of a play in which Inge was probably at his experimental best although artistically his experiment fell short of success. Typical of the comments about the play is that by John Gassner: "The Jewish cadet's drama was dragged in, and the play, sometimes veering towards comedy and sometimes toward tragedy, was inconsistent in tone."[28] What Professor Gassner says undeniably has point; however, Inge specifically strove toward what has

*All references to *The Dark at the Top of the Stairs* will be to the first edition of the work, published by Random House in 1958.

seemed to many to be an inconsistency in tone. He is writing essentially about the Cora-Rubin conflict in this play and about the isolation which it imposes upon the members of the Flood family. The conflict reaches a peak in the first act when Rubin quarrels with Cora because she has plotted behind his back to buy their daughter Reenie a new dress. Cora goads Rubin into striking her, and he leaves with an avowal not to return.

In the early stages of Act II, attention is divided. Cora is entertaining her sister, Lottie, and her brother-in-law, Morris, at dinner; she is much concerned with her present marital plight and attempts to persuade Lottie and Morris to let her and the children come to Oklahoma City to live with them. She is also immediately concerned during this act with getting Reenie ready to go to the country-club party which the newly rich Ralstons are giving for their daughter, Mary Jane. The high point in the act is the arrival on the scene of Reenie's date, Sammy Goldenbaum, who is accompanied by another couple, Punky Givens and Flirt. Sammy is an appealing character on stage, even though he is a bit too good to seem real. Sammy, whose appearance is confined to a brief portion of Act II, is a central character. When he and the other young people exit, Cora and her guests return to a discussion of the marital situation which faces Cora; but this concluding material is distinctly anti-climactic. The play's real climax is reached in the middle of Act III when Flirt appears on the scene with the news that Sammy Goldenbaum has committed suicide. However, this climax is followed almost immediately by a secondary climax in which Inge turns attention to the original conflict between Rubin and Cora by having Rubin return in an attempt to mend his differences with Cora. Rubin symbolically enters the house without his customary boots, explaining to Cora that they are muddy, that "I din wanta track up your nice, clean house" (97). This sign is the first that he, like other Inge males, is being domesticated.

To some people, the divided emphasis in this play was disconcerting, especially since the major conflict is not the one in which the major climax occurs. Inge explains his technique by saying, "I deliberately divert the audience from the main story in order to bring them back to it at the end of the play with a fresher viewpoint. In the play, I try to explore some of man's hidden fear in facing life and to show something of the hidden fears that motivate us all."[29] Superficially, Sammy's suicide is the climax of the Sammy-versus-Society conflict; but examined more closely, it must be acknowledged that the suicide is the act which brings Cora and Reenie to a new realization of the meaning of life and to a new understanding of themselves.

But Inge does not do a perfect job of relating the two parts of the play. The suicide in itself is not entirely convincing, nor does Inge argue away the objections to it by stating, "Some people felt . . . that the announcement of the suicide came as too much of a shock; but every suicide I ever heard of came to me in the same way, with no preparation. I have never heard of a suicide I expected."[30] Inge perhaps errs in trying to explain and defend Sammy's suicide on realistic grounds. The suicide is, first, more successful as a symbol than as a reality; and, secondly, it serves a very useful function in bringing about the resolution of the play. It is justified on artistic grounds, and any other justification does not seem necessary or appropriate. Had Inge prepared for the suicide by making Sammy a morose and maudlin figure, the rash act would have been more convincing realistically; but the audience would then have made no closer an identification with Sammy than it did with Punky Givens, the other young cadet, who remains slinkingly in the background and mumbles unintelligbly whenever he is called upon to speak. Inge describes Punky as "a disappointment as a human being" (53), and he portrays him in a generally unfavorable light to provide contrast to Sammy's warm and glowing personality and to force the audience to experience extremes of feelings about both the cadets.

The dark at the top of the stairs, from which the play's title is derived, is realistically staged. Inge's directions call for a flight of stairs at the far left of the stage: "At the top of them is the upstairs hallway, which is not accessible to windows and sunlight. During the daytime scenes, this small area is in semidarkness, and at night it is black. When the hallway is lighted, we can see the feet of the characters who happen to be there." Inge continues with a sentence in which the symbolic impact of the dark area is made clear: "We are conscious of this area throughout the play, as though it holds some possible threat to the characters" (3). Just as Little Sheba became a symbol of lost youth and lost innocence in *Come Back, Little Sheba,* the dark at the top of the stairs comes in this play to be a representation of the fear that all men feel. This meaning is made abundantly clear in the dialogue. Cora asks Sonny, who does not want to go upstairs alone, "Sonny, why are you so afraid of the dark?" Sonny replies, "'cause . . . you can't see what's in front of you. And it might be something awful" (79). At the second act curtain, Cora and Sonny go up the stairs together "to face the darkness hovering there like an omen."

When Rubin has lost his job selling harness, he comes home and finally tells Cora of his plight; he says that he is going to take another job, this time selling machinery. Then he reveals his fears about the future: "I'm scared. I don't know how I'll make out. I . . . I'm scared," to which Cora responds, "I never supposed you had it *in* you to fear." Rubin launches into a lengthy speech regarding the changes which have taken place during his life—these include the increasing popularity of the automobile which makes Rubin's job of selling harness obsolete —and ends his speech, "I'm a stranger in the very land I was born in" (100-1).

Rubin, too, is afraid of the dark, because it represents the future and uncertainty. But just as Cora assuages Sonny's fear of the dark by going up the stairs with him at the end of Act II, so does she assuage Rubin's fear of the dark (future) by going upstairs to him at the third-act curtain. And this time there is light at the top of the stairs where Rubin stands waiting. The parallelism between the endings of these two acts also marks the beginning, presumably, of a more healthy relationship between Cora and Rubin. Inge means to suggest that the Oedipus problems between Cora and Sonny are now done with and that Cora's marriage, long threatened by these problems, will now return to normal. However, this suggestion is difficult to accept in view of the objective evidence throughout the play of the formidable Oedipus situation.

Throughout the play, Inge consciously builds toward an understanding and clear statement of the Oedipus problem. It is clear very early that Rubin's frequent absence from home makes Cora very unhappy. She tells him: "I envy women who have their husbands with them all the time. I never have anyone to take me any place. I live like a widow" (5). Cora's only real companionship is with her children, and she tends to romanticize it because it is all she has. It is also obvious that Rubin has little real feeling for his children, partly because Cora has been so possessive of them that he has thought himself unable to compete for their affection; he accuses Cora of possessiveness in no uncertain terms when he shocks her by saying, "You're like an old mare Pa used to have on the ranch. Never wanted to give up her colts. By God, she'd keep 'em locked inside her and make all us men dig inside her with our hands to get 'em out. She never wanted to let 'em go" (7). Rubin says clearly what he thinks when he tells Cora, "You're always kissin' and makin' over the boy until I sometimes wonder who's top man around here" (6). By the end of Act II, there is no question about who has this position at that moment; Cora tells Sonny, "You're the man of the house now, Sonny. You mustn't be afraid" (79).

Sonny's jealousy of his father is another important factor in the development of the Oedipus situation. It is obvious that Sonny wishes him to remain away; for, when Cora tries to reach Rubin by long distance telephone, Sonny says, "I bet he isn't there. I bet anything" (78). Sonny is correct; Rubin is not there. Cora is described as having "A fallen expression on her face" until she hears a car outside, whereupon she dashes to the window. Again Sonny expresses his subconscious wish to have his father out of the way by saying, "It isn't Dad. I can always tell the sound of his car" (79). And when Rubin strikes Cora and leaves, all that Sonny can do is jump up and down in glee shouting, "Goody, goody, goody. I want to move to Oklahoma City" (33).

The Oedipus problem is suggested again by Sammy, who is giving his autobiography in a single speech which runs over half a page in print and which is the longest speech in the play. He has told about his mother and about her many marriages. He has indicated his utter isolation from anyone for whom he might be expected to care. But he then tells of two idyllic days which he spent with his mother in San Francisco—"She let me take her to dinner and to a show and to dance. Just like we were sweethearts. It was the most wonderful time I ever had. And then I had to go back to the old military academy" (63).

The resolution of the Oedipus problem is suggested in an especially tense encounter between Cora and Sonny. Cora confronts the problem when she says, "Sonny, you mustn't come crawling into my bed any more. I let you do it last night, but I shouldn't have. It was wrong." Sonny explains, "I was scared." But Cora is firm and replies, "Just the same, that's not to happen again, Sonny. It's not the same when a boy your age comes crawling into bed with his mother. You can't expect me to mean as much to you as when you were a baby. . . . I think you're older in your feelings than I ever realized. You're a funny mixture, Sonny. In some ways, shy as your sister. In other ways, bold as a pirate" (90). This awkward encounter soon gives way to the play's most climactic scene—Flirt's revelation that Sammy has killed himself—which provides tragic relief from the intensity of the Sonny-Cora encounter.

Cora's frank conversation with Sonny takes place right after Sonny has returned from giving a recitation for which he has been paid five dollars. This is the first money the boy has earned, and he wants to use part of it to go to a movie and to buy a big sundae afterward. But Cora takes the money from him and puts it into his piggy bank despite his violent protests. Sonny goes into a virtual tantrum—one of several which he suffers in the course of the play. Described as "wild at the injustice," he shouts at his mother: "Look what you've done. I hate you! I wanta see the movie. I've just gotta see the movie. If I can't see the movie, I'll kill myself" (89). Inge attempts to bring about the final resolution of the Oedipus problem when Sonny, in the last minutes of the play, takes his piggy bank and tells Reenie: "I don't care. She's not going to boss me for the rest of my life. It's *my* money, and I've got a right to spend it" (107). He then dashes the bank against the fireplace. This action represents Sonny's emancipation, his emergence as a man; however, the solution not only is too pat but happens over too short a period to be any more convincing than is the oversimplified resolution of the Oedipus problem in *A Loss of Roses* in which one night of illicit love supposedly emancipates the twenty-one-year-old son.

All of Inge's major plays have strong Oedipus overtones, excluding possibly *Bus Stop*. Both Lola in *Come Back, Little Sheba* and Lottie in *The Dark at the Top of the Stairs* are mother-wife figures, while in *Picnic* Madge is a mother-mistress figure. *A Loss of Roses* is a full-fledged excursion into Thebes; and in *Natural Affection* Donnie's Oedipal jealousy becomes the major wedge between Sue Barker and Bernie Slovenk. Inge's women, as Robert Brustein has ably pointed out, want to tame their men—to make sons of them, as it were. And none of Inge's men really rebels against this except Rubin who in *The Dark at the Top of the Stairs*, walks out. But Rubin's rebellion, one must presume, is short-lived. Rubin is "always afraid of endin' up like . . . your brother-in-law Morris" (102), and Inge does not present a very good case for his ending up otherwise. Nor will a night in bed alter the futility of the Flood's future. Rubin is still out of a job, and he is still not ready to settle down into the sort of situation which would bring him closer to his family. Even at the end of the play, he is unable to communicate with his son, and it is doubtful that he ever will find grounds for communicating. One must, in all honesty, admit that the bulk of the damage in the Flood family has been done and that it is probably too late for any panacea to take effect. Reenie, even though she now recognizes her own selfishness, stands only a remote chance of ever finding anyone with whom she can really share her life, for her childhood has left her too much on the defensive. She tells her mother: "I don't think I ever want to get married. . . . I don't want to fight with anyone, like you and Daddy" (86).

Reenie is very much like Laura Wingfield in *Glass Menagerie*. *Farther Off From Heaven*, of which *The Dark at the Top of the Stairs* is an extension, was written when Williams' direct influence upon Inge was very strong. In the early play, Reenie, like Laura, had a physical imperfection of which she was keenly aware—one of her front teeth was broken. This helped to explain her almost pathological shyness, one so acute that the thought of going to Mary Jane Ralston's party with Sammy made her sick to her stomach. But even without an obvious physical imperfection, Reenie's shyness is easily explainable in terms of her background. Just as Laura sought to escape by means of her glass animals, Reenie attempts to escape by playing the piano; and a point is made of telling the audience that she will not perform before anyone, that she plays just for herself, a fact which clearly indicates that music is her means of escape. When she at one point becomes jealous of the affection which Cora lavishes upon Sonny, "Reenie looks disdainfully at them, and marches into the parlor, where, in a moment, we hear her playing a lovely Chopin nocturne" (34).

Reenie's shyness is indirectly responsible for Sammy's suicide. So upset was she by Mary Jane Ralston's party that she fled from it without seeking Sammy out to tell him that she was leaving. Flirt tells Reenie, "The other kids told me Sammy was looking for you everywhere. He was going around asking everyone, 'Where's Reenie?'" (93). When Cora comprehends the situation, she deals with Reenie very passionately: "I've heard all I intend to listen to about being so shy and sensitive and afraid of people. I can't respect those feelings any more. They're nothing but selfishness" (95). The situation now is crystallized for Reenie who says, in considerable misery, "He asked for *me* . . . for *me*. The only time anyone ever *wanted* me, or *needed* me, in my entire life. And I wasn't there. I didn't stop once to think of . . . Sammy. I've always thought I was the only person in the world who had any feelings at all" (96). The change which Sammy's suicide brings about in Reenie is symbolized by her saying to Rubin, "I've been practicing a new piece, Daddy. It's Chopin. Do you want me to play it for you?" (104). For the first time, Reenie is using her music not as a form of escape but as a form of bringing someone else pleasure.

Cora has faced life quite unrealistically throughout her marriage, but Rubin's frequent absence has increased in her the necessity to romanticize. She is being most unrealistic when she talks of moving in with Lottie and Morris and of finding a job in Oklahoma City. Even assuming that she found a job—and with her lack of experience and education, this would not be a justifiable assumption—she could hardly hope to maintain a home and to support the children on what she might earn. An example of her tendency to romanticize is also found in the remarks she makes to imply that Sammy has come all the way from California just for a date with Reenie—a blind date, at that (45)—when in actuality he has just come from a neighboring town where he is a student in the military academy. But there is little evidence that Cora can face any sort of reality for more than a few minutes at a time. Certainly she should know Rubin well enough to realize that he would never be content in the sort of job she envisions for him—running a corner grocery or being manager of a neighborhood chain store. Yet it seems that this is the sort of thing which she will surely push him toward. Despite sporadic efforts on Inge's part to make Cora seem to be more realistic, she still remains the romanticist who feels "I could give them [Sonny and Reenie] life like a present, all wrapped in white, with every promise of happiness inside"; she will feel the same way tomorrow even though for the nonce she can say to Rubin, "All I can promise them now is life itself" (103).

The most confused person in *The Dark at the Top of the Stairs* is Lottie; indeed, her suicide would have been much more convincing than Sammy's in the light of what is revealed about each character in the play. Lottie's basic problem is two-pronged: She is obviously sex-starved, and she has the simultaneous desire to master and to be mastered. In a sense she is reminiscent of Rosemary in *Picnic*. Through the years Lottie has become a gross and vulgar woman. She stuffs herself with food—"she reaches for the bag of fried chicken. . . . She brings out a gizzard to gnaw on" (77)—and she most indecorously removes her corset in public and, rubbing her great fleshy stomach, proclaims, "My God! That feels good" (76-77). Lottie claims to be disappointed by sex—"I never did enjoy it the way some women—say they do" (75). But for one who finds sex so disappointing, she is remarkably concerned that "it's been over three years since he [Morris] even touched me" (72). It is also obvious that Lottie enjoys her fantasies of other men and that she never admits to herself the psychological overtones of these fantasies. She protests the suggestion that Rudolph Valentino is one of her favorite movie stars and claims to have seen *The Sheik* four times only "because Marietta Flagmeyer wanted me to keep her company" (49). But in the next breath she says: "You know, it scares me a little to look at him [Valentino]. Those eyes, that seem to be laughing at you, and all those white teeth. I think it's a sin for a man to be as pretty as he is. Why, I'd be scared to death to let a man like him touch me" (50).

Lottie is also quite ambivalent in her feelings toward Rubin. She tells of how Cora first saw him "riding down the street on a shiny black horse," and she adds, "My God, he was handsome" (43). Then she admits liking Rubin and tells Morris: "He's made a lot better husband than I ever thought he would. But I'm glad *I'm* not married to him. I'd be worried to death all the time. I'm glad I'm married to a nice man I can trust." Having thus reassured herself that her interest in Rubin is purely objective, she can later say to Cora: "My God, a big handsome buck like Rubin! Who cares if he's honorable?" (71)—and then tell Cora a clearly phallic joke.

Lottie represents the unhappy combination of vulgarity, puritanism, self-righteousness, and bigotry which is so often found in severely repressed individuals. So extreme is her bigotry that it is ludicrous. She tells Morris: "Maybe you'd like to marry Norma Talmadge someday and then let the Pope tell you what to do the rest of your life, making you swear to leave all your money to the church, and bring up all your children Catholic, and then join the Knights of Columbus and take an oath to go out and kill all the nice Protestant women when the day comes for the Catholics to take over the world" (48). Still believing firmly in the existence of a church militant, Lottie tells wild tales which have come to her third hand by way of Marietta Flagmeyer of how the Catholics keep arsenals in their church basements, stashed there against the day when the Catholics take over the world. She is also anti-Semitic; but, when she meets Sammy Goldenbaum, she tells him, "Why, we don't think a thing about a person's being Jewish, do we, Morris?" (57), and then proceeds to advise him to join the Christian Science Church because she knows a former Jewish woman in Oklahoma City who was very unhappy, "But she joined the Christian Science church and has been perfectly happy ever since" (57).

Lottie feels totally unfulfilled as a women. She complains that she has no children, only a house full of cats. When Cora says, "You always claimed you never wanted children," Lottie replies, quite touchingly, "Well . . . what else can I say to people?" (69).

Lottie finally gives Cora the message which Inge delivers in all his plays: "Call up Rubin and ask him to come back. Beg him to come back, if you have to get down on your knees" (70).

It is clear that Cora's marriage to Rubin—a marriage which is some seventeen years old when the action of the play opens—has been based almost wholly upon physical attraction, and that this attraction still holds it somewhat uncertainly together. Cora was pregnant by Rubin within two weeks of her first meeting with him. It is apparent that there is very little common ground between the two except in the bedroom. The complete breakdown in communication between them is apparent early in the play. Cora is so imperceptive of her husband that she does not realize—or has never admitted to herself—that he is capable of fear. She is so insecure basically that she cannot admit Rubin's inmost weaknesses.

Cora, again acting out of basic insecurity, attempts to dictate to Rubin. When he has returned home in good faith to beg her forgiveness after he has struck her, he startles her; and her first words to him are "Rubin! I hate to be frightened so" (97). Within a few speeches, during which Rubin reveals to her the gravity of his present situation, Cora is again dictating, telling him that he cannot accept another traveling job and that he must talk with John Fraser about finding a job in a local market. Rubin, in his most forceful speech in the play, tells her: "Don't you realize you can't talk to a man like that? Don't you realize that every time you talk that way, I just gotta go out and raise more hell, just to prove to myself I'm a free man? . . . All these years we been married, you never once really admitted to yourself what kinda man I am." And Rubin sums up with this statement his seventeen years of futility: "No, ya keep talkin' to me like I was the kinda man you think I *oughta* be. Look at me. Don't you know who I am? Don't you know who I am?" (99).

In *The Theme of Loneliness in Modern American Drama*, Winifred Dusenbury claims that Arthur Miller's chief concern in *Death of a Salesman* is with the question of how the Loman family became separated.[31] Such, too, is Inge's concern in *The Dark at the Top of the Stairs*. Rubin's separation from his children is partly an outgrowth of his feeling of alienation from his society—"How can I feel I've got anything to give to my

children when the world's as strange to me as it is to them?"
(101)—but it is also very directly connected with his wife's feeling of separation from him. Because he is away so much and
because he is a virtual stranger to her when he is at home, Cora
reaches out clutchingly toward her children, especially toward
Sonny. But there is no real spiritual communication between
Cora and the children. When Cora most needs them and when
she most fears being alone, Reenie retreats to the piano and
Sonny to the movies or to his pictures of movie stars.

Until the very end of the play, Reenie and Sonny are almost
completely cut off from each other. They bicker in a way that
far exceeds the usual sibling rivalry in well-adjusted families.
Their bickering is simply an extension of the behavior patterns
which they have witnessed in their parents, and the implication
is strong that the man-versus-woman contention which they have
been brought up with will make life adjustment very difficult,
if not impossible, for them. The fact that Reenie and Sonny go
off to the movies together at the end of the play certainly cannot convince one that a transformation has taken place and that
from this day forward the basic contention between them is going
to be replaced by sympathy and understanding. They will be
back at the same old stands tomorrow, fighting like two Killarney
cats; and their bickering alone—even assuming that Cora and
Rubin might come to a better understanding of each other—
will be enough to drive Rubin back to the relative peace and
harmony of the road.

Cora's separation from her family is heightened by the cold-
ness with which Lottie receives her request that she share her
home with Cora and the children. In this scene—even though
Lottie does relent most reluctantly at the end—one is reminded
of the rejection which Lola receives in *Come Back, Little Sheba*
when she calls her mother to ask whether she might come home.
In both cases, negative forces serve to bring about the domestic
reunion; whether such negative forces can give impetus to a
force so positive as love is highly doubtful. When people have
lived in spiritual isolation for seventeen years, as Cora and
Rubin have, it is unrealistic to project a simple solution for their
difficulties. Inge attempts to use sex as the great leveler much

as Williams does with Stella and Stanley in *A Streetcar Named Desire;* however, Williams was realistic enough to portray Stella and Stanley during the early years of their marriage. After seventeen years together, the Kowalski's would probably have had to use something other than sex to get "them colored lights goin'."

In the character of Sonny, Inge presents one of the most memorable brats in modern American drama. There is scarcely a moment during which one would not like to throttle the child. His tantrums have generally led his mother to yield to him, and her doing so has made him realize the effectiveness of temper and has led him to newer and more effective displays of it. Judging from one of Lottie's lines in the play—"Mama and Papa were no match for her [Cora] when she wanted her own way" (43)—Sonny's resoluteness has been honestly come by.

Sonny's ability to recite does not serve to endear him to an audience already hard put to find any good qualities in him. His recitations separate him from other children of his age and suggest exhibitionism rather than ability. The one recitation to which the audience is exposed is, significantly, Hamlet's soliloquy (61) which reinforces the Oedipus overtones of the play and which also introduces the question of suicide around which so much of the latter part of the play revolves.

Dramatically and structurally one must say that *The Dark at the Top of the Stairs* is slightly out of focus and somewhat out of control. Sammy's suicide is too dramatic, and it diverts attention too impellingly from the conflicts within the Flood family to be dramatically justifiable. Inge's basic idea of diverting attention from the main plot of the play so that it could be approached at the end with renewed perspective was splendid. However, the suicide is revealed so close to the ending and with such impact that the author is unable to achieve anything in the main plot which begins to equal it climactically. As the story is told, Sammy's suicide is more believable than many critics have indicated. The focus of the play is intentionally placed upon the Floods; only in the second act do outsiders intrude upon the family—even Flirt's appearance in acts I and III serves the sole function of providing the audience with necessary information. But Inge brings Sammy's spirit into the third act as the most pervasive force in the first half of the act, only to drop him clumsily in the second half of the act in order that he can return to the original plot and bring about its resolution. It seems totally incredible that Rubin, upon his return, should be told nothing about Sammy's suicide and that the family should return to its routine so easily.

Many members of the theater audience agreed with John Gassner who "had little stomach for comedy after observing the suffering of the children and experiencing the penumbral mood of the scenes just past. It was impossible for me to put them out of mind in watching the facile resolution."[32] Gassner also points out with considerable insight that "his [Inge's] group play technique tends to dissolve this central drama in favor of peripheral themes, chiefly the mistakes that women make in trying to run men's lives. Everything Inge shows us here seems to be authentic, but his several truths weaken the one truth."[33] This criticism applies equally to *Picnic* and *Bus Stop* in which the author allows his themes to develop too permissively and in which too many minor themes are pursued when they are suggested by the major theme.

The Dark at the Top of the Stairs has been criticized by some because it depends so heavily upon clichés. Such criticism is unjust, for the people of whom Inge is writing do ninety per cent of their thinking and speaking in clichés. Were he to present them in any other way, he could justly be accused of presenting unrealistic and unconvincing dialogue. More valid, however, is the claim that some of the dialogue is contrived. Lottie's garrulousness is used, as Lola's was in *Come Back, Little Sheba*, to provide background for the action; but the telling is so direct and so sustained that the author's guiding hand becomes all too evident.

Despite its imperfections, *The Dark at the Top of the Stairs* is one of the most sensitive and perceptive presentations of the quest of the little man to find identity in his society that has yet come to the American stage. Inge's forthrightness and delicacy endear him to audiences. His work is, as Richard Hayes has aptly put it, "full of the pleasures of recognition."[34]

V *Success, the Bitch Goddess*

It is not unusual for authors to score notable successes early in their careers. Robert Sherwood staked his claim to Broadway recognition with the successful and rollicking satire *The Road to Rome* in 1927; but he was not to produce another play of comparable stature until the 1932 production of *Reunion in Vienna*. Clifford Odets was to skyrocket to fame and recognition in 1935 when *Waiting for Lefty* and *Awake and Sing!* were produced within four months of each other. Robert Anderson was to make his mark in 1953 with the production of *Tea and Sympathy* only to fade into obscurity after the production of two commercial failures, *All Summer Long* in 1954, and *Silent Night, Lonely Night* in 1959. Thomas Wolfe told his basic story in its entirety in *Look Homeward, Angel* and *Of Time and the River*, his first two books, only to repeat it with variations in his later, less successful work. Reynolds Price has made his mark with a first novel, *A Long and Happy Life;* and he must now work toward fulfilling the destiny which the critics have predicted for him.

William Inge rode the crest of a wave from 1950 until 1959, and this is a truly remarkable feat. Each of his new plays represented a new high-water mark for him; and, unlike the careers of Miller and Williams and O'Neill, Inge's career advanced steadily, unabatedly, for nearly a decade. But a decade of success, especially so early in one's career, tends to turn a playwright into something of a public monument, and once the tradition of success is established, the public presses an author toward further production, ever challenging him to improve upon himself. And when the established author falls short, he can either make a Steinbeck-like rationalization—So I wrote a potboiler!—and leave the door open for his next really artistic creation; or he can strike out against a fickle public and defend his work as Inge did after the failure of *A Loss of Roses*.

Robert Brustein has referred to Inge as a "fiddle with one string."[35] This cliché is sufficiently applicable to Inge for many people to accept it as truth. However, Inge has actually been writing variations on a theme, and each variation has had freshness. One cannot always easily agree with Inge's suggestion that modern man's redemption is through sex; however, as any sociologist or psychologist knows, a significant number of unlikely relationships are perpetuated on a sexual basis and in many marriages sex appears to be the only common ground between two people.

The time has now come for Inge to assert himself, to turn a deaf ear to many of his critics, and to write instinctively with the sort of strength which he achieved in *Come Back, Little Sheba.* His instincts may sometimes betray him, but a study of the effects which criticism has had upon his work, especially upon *A Loss of Roses* and *Natural Affection,* points undeniably to the fact that those who have sought to help him have often unwittingly betrayed him more than his sound artistic instincts would have been likely to.

CHAPTER 3

And By the Wind Grieved, Ghost

"I like things always to be
sweet as possible."
—Lila in *A Loss of Roses*

INGE'S MOST DIFFICULT YEARS since his arrival on
Broadway have been those from 1959 to 1963. During this
period Inge produced two plays, *A Loss of Roses* and *Natural
Affection*, both of which were to receive not merely unfavorable
reviews, but in many cases scathing ones. This chapter is concerned with these two plays and with the Inge scenario,
Splendor in the Grass, which was written in 1961 and for which
Inge was honored with an Academy Award in 1962. *A Loss of
Roses*, rewritten and brought into sharper focus, was to be made
into a Twentieth Century-Fox film entitled *The Stripper*, which
was considerably more successful than the Broadway play.

The almost unanimous rejection of *A Loss of Roses* by both
critics and audiences had a profound effect upon the author.
Inge had once written that some very vital part of an author goes
into what he writes and that "if it is rejected, he can only feel
that he is rejected, too. Some part of him has been turned down,
cast aside, even laughed at or scorned."[1] This statement, written
more than a year before *A Loss of Roses* came to Broadway,
was to seem more cogent after the production of this play than it
had been before it; for Inge had never experienced a failure
until then. When the first New York reviews of his fifth major
play had been published, Inge, who had had reservations about

bringing the play to New York in the state in which it finally appeared, left New York and made an impetuous journey to Nashville, not like a petulant child, but like someone who had been beaten down and who had temporarily lost his identity. He fled to Nashville to recover from the disappointment which attended the opening of his play and to restore that part of his personality which had been lacerated by the personal attacks which some of the critics made upon him. Inge, who had spent almost a decade in New York, now felt the need to escape from a city which had always been somewhat alien to him and which now struck him as being blatantly hostile. He also needed a freedom which New York, because of its geographical constriction, could not offer him, and he needed a freedom of technique which stage writing could not offer him. It is not surprising, therefore, that he was soon in Hollywood writing for the films.

Splendor in the Grass, an outstanding scenario in many important respects, is discussed in this chapter dealing with two Broadway productions because such a presentation enables the reader to see the contrasts between Inge's scenario and stage writing. Inge used his new medium to its full advantage, reveling in its fluidity. He was like the sculptor who switches from marble to clay or the painter who switches from water colors to oils. Now, not bound by the static scenery of the stage, Inge was able to move gracefully from scene to scene. He was also less bound by the unity of time of which he was especially conscious in most of his Broadway writing. Only in *A Loss of Roses* does as much as a month elapse between significant portions of the action. *Come Back, Little Sheba* takes place essentially in a twenty-four hour period, although the anticlimax, Doc's return from the hospital, takes place two weeks after the main action of the play. *Picnic* is closely confined to a twenty-four hour period, and *Bus Stop* is still more closely confined to a five hour period. *The Dark at the Top of the Stairs* is necessarily extended to a period of one week so that Rubin can leave his family and return to it. However, *Splendor in the Grass* covers a period of several years and represents Inge's totally new approach to the unfolding of his story. The absence of the controls which are evident in his first four major plays is not operative in his scenario, symbolizing the new freedom the author was seeking.

It appeared for a time that Inge would remain in Hollywood, especially after the publication of an interview in which he claimed to be totally disenchanted by New York and completely captivated by California.[2] However, before 1962 was ended, he had returned to New York to see his new play, *Natural Affection*, put into production. It opened at the Booth on January 31, 1963, and it proved disastrous commercially. It was a rare critic who did not have some good things to say about the play; however, the critics felt almost unanimously that the first half of the play, which had a satisfactory pace and in which suspense was well built, was severely weakened and to a large extent negated by the sensationalism in the latter half.

One can only speculate on what reception *A Loss of Roses* and *Natural Affection* might have received had they been Inge's first two plays. It is highly probable that the former would not have been produced until it had been rewritten with Lila as the central character, and this would have done much toward strengthening the play. Having rewritten the play in this way, Inge would probably have been heralded as a rising young playwright. *A Loss of Roses* would not have brought him the plaudits that *Come Back, Little Sheba* had, but it is likely that it would have paved the way solidly toward future productions.

Natural Affection, despite some of its profoundly moving vignettes, is merely suggestive of the author's gifts; and, as an early work in the Inge canon, it would have been an indication of promising potentiality. Unfortunately, many have looked upon the play, coming as it did after four major successes and one failure, as the death knell of a not inconsiderable talent. It is, however, much too early to judge Inge with any really intelligent perspective.

I A Loss of Roses*

A Loss of Roses chronicles the depression of the human spirit. If Inge has been adversely criticized for pursuing a redemption-through-sex theme in his earlier plays, he must now be chided for presenting a play in which sex does not really suggest

---

* All references to *A Loss of Roses* are to the Bantam edition of the book (Bantam Book # J2490) which was published in 1963. The original Random House edition was published in 1960.

redemption in any convincing or satisfying way. Sex does crystallize the basic Oedipus problems of two of the principals in the play, and the audience is meant to be left with the feeling that perhaps Kenny's one night of love with Lila has provided him with a means of solving this problem; but, if the audience is given such a feeling, it must be admitted that the author has been guilty of oversimplification. Inge here, as in his other plays, gives the audience false hope; for Kenny's umbilicus is made of tougher stuff than the play suggests at its conclusion.

Inge's presentation of the Oedipus complex, which is of the greatest significance in *The Dark at the Top of the Stairs,* is the central psychological concern of *A Loss of Roses.* The central male character in the play, Kenny, is twenty-one years old and is in many respects Sonny Flood come of age. The sibling rivalry which somewhat sharpened the lines of the conflict in *The Dark at the Top of the Stairs*—Reenie suggests the Electra conflict in this play—is missing from *A Loss of Roses.* However, by doing away with sibling rivalry and by making Kenny an only child, Inge gains more ground than he loses. In the first place, he avoids the annoying sort of bickering which took place between Sonny and Reenie in the earlier play; and he is more fully in control of the mounting tensions between mother and son in the later play because these tensions are not diluted as they often were by Reenie in *The Dark at the Top of the Stairs.* But herein is part of Inge's problem in *A Loss of Roses*—the focus is more on Kenny and Helen Baird than is desirable. Inge gives Lila approximately equivalent dramatic status with Kenny and Helen; and, as has been suggested, his play would be much stronger if Lila had unquestionably been the major character, which she was in the film version.

If *A Loss of Roses* is largely the story of an only child, it is certainly the story of an only child who has two mothers. If Inge is to succeed in making his presentation of the psychological conflicts in the play convincing, he must create in Lila a woman who is at once attractive and alluring, but who is quite a bit older than Kenny—she is thirty-two years old in the play. He makes his portrayal more convincing by casting Lila as an actress who early in the action demonstrates her ability to attract men. She is introduced as being partially a representation of love fulfillment—"She is an extraordinarily beautiful woman . . . blond and voluptuous"—and partially as a representation of a surrogate mother: "One feels immediately a sincerity about her and a generosity of spirit" (22). The point of Lila's being a surrogate mother is emphasized throughout the play by the reiteration of the fact that Lila used to look after Kenny when he was a baby and a small child—and this explanation is somewhat less than convincing inasmuch as Lila would have been only eleven or twelve years old when Kenny was a baby. However, one of Lila's early speeches leads directly into the establishment of the surrogate mother image which Inge's audience must accept if his play is to have point. Lila tells Kenny: "I bet you don't remember me much, do you? Your Aunt Lila? . . . I used to look after you when you were a baby. I fed you your bottle and changed your didies, and bounced you on my knee to keep you from crying. I was kind of a substitute mother for you, Kenny. But I loved you like you were my own" (24). And later Kenny significantly reminisces when he informs Lila: "I'm beginning to remember more about you now, Lila. The way you took care of me when I was a kid. Mom was kinda strict but you'd gimme anything I wanted" (41). The situation basically has not changed a jot from what Kenny remembers it as having been in the past. Lila is permissive throughout the play: she waits on Kenny, she keeps his secrets, she feels empathy with him when Helen's rejection of his anniversary gift upsets him severely; and she eventually capitulates to his advances after he has been hurt by his mother and after she has deluded herself into believing that Kenny might marry her.

The characters in *A Loss of Roses* are presented as having less conscious awareness of the Oedipus situation than Cora Flood had in *The Dark at the Top of the Stairs*. It is true that early in the play Helen, who "withdraws from Kenny like a shy maiden" when he tries to kiss her, says, "You're too old to still be making love to me like you did when you were a baby" (13); but more often a direct acknowledgment of the basic Oedipus issue is skirted by the characters or is suggested by means of *double-entendres* such as that found in the dialogue between Lila and Helen after Kenny has given his mother a wrist watch for her wedding anniversary and she has rejected the gift:

HELEN: I can't let him do the things his father did, Lila.

LILA: But every boy wants to be like his father.

HELEN: There are some ways he can't be allowed.

LILA: But a *present* . . . that he wanted to *give* you.

HELEN: I couldn't take it.

LILA: You can be hard, Helen.

HELEN: Yes. When I have to be.

LILA: I could never be hard that way.

HELEN: We pay for our weaknesses.

LILA: Yes. You have to be hard to be good, don't you?

(81-82)

This portion of dialogue serves two significant functions. In the first place, it indicates Helen's recognition, conscious or subconscious, of the existence of the Oedipus problem; and, in the second, it prepares the audience for Lila's final capitulation to Kenny—"I could never be hard that way." This statement is not the only preparation the audience is given for what is to occur between Kenny and Lila; indeed, the entire play is built up to this climax rather calculatedly. Often Inge, in building toward his climax, uses his details secondarily to illustrate the problems which exist between Helen and Kenny and to make the existence of them more convincing. Lila has been on stage only a few moments when she observes to Helen, "You know, when I first saw him [Kenny] standing there, I thought for a moment he was big Kenneth. They look so much alike" (23). This observation comes immediately to mind when, later in the play, Lila confesses to Helen: "I had the wildest crush on your husband that a silly, young girl could possibly have" (32). It becomes clear at this point that Lila's crush is going to be transferred to Kenny, and Lila's earlier statement helps to explain some of Helen's own fears in regard to her son.

Helen and Kenny bicker perpetually throughout the play, but the bickering has more point here than it had in *The Dark at the Top of the Stairs*. It indicates the tensions which have built up between Helen and her son, and it also serves to illustrate the strong love which exists between them, for most of their quarrels are resolved by some display or affirmation of affection.

Helen fights her own possessiveness in the play; she wants to be independent, and she has convinced herself that she wants to free Kenny to live his own life. However, her nagging is just a manifestation of the possessiveness she cannot overcome.

Helen has cause to be resentful of Kenny, and her resentment occasionally comes to the fore, although it is usually present only indirectly in the bickering. In essence, Kenny has twice deprived Helen of the fulfillment which she might find in love and marriage. It was in saving Kenny from drowning that Helen's husband was drowned. After she had been a widow for some time—there is a contradiction of time in the play at this point, for Kenny was said to be a freshman, presumably about age fourteen, when his father died (34), but is later pictured as being nine or ten years old a year or two after his father's death (53)—Helen had the opportunity to marry another man but she did not do so because "Kenny hated him" (52).

In a very real sense, Kenny is more possessive of his mother than she is of him. His objection to her remarrying illustrates this in part, but his continued possessiveness is seen in his desire to have her stop working and stay at home—to be largely dependent upon him. And the very things that Kenny wants of his mother come to be supplied by Lila who washes Kenny's socks and cooks elaborate meals. Lila's taking over such duties continually emphasizes her role as surrogate mother, and Inge never ceases to strengthen this image of her. At one point, for example, he has Lila say: "You don't have to apologize to *me*, Kenny. I'm not your mother." Kenny's answer, "Yah. I forgot" (41) is fraught with meaning. And later Helen says to Lila: "You're just what he's been waiting for. Another mother to pamper him" (76).

The watch symbol is especially vital to the psychological impact of the play. It would have been well for Inge to have done more with this symbol and to have scrapped the contrived and seemingly tacked-on symbol of the roses at the end of the play. In one of her reminiscences with Lila, Helen says, "I've still got the watch he [her husband, Kenneth] gave me for our fifth anniversary" (32). The audience is later told that this watch, now probably seventeen or eighteen years old, has stopped working and that Helen intends to have it repaired. But the high point of the play's action is led into when Kenny spends over fifty dollars to buy his mother a new watch for her anniversary which she still celebrates because "It's one of the few things in the world I have to celebrate" (73). Lila has prepared a festive dinner for the occasion and has even mixed some drinks. When Kenny comes home, he shows her the package which he has for his mother, as well as the receipt for the watch.

In the beginning of Act II, before Helen arrives home for her anniversary dinner, one has the feeling that Lila and Kenny are playing house like two children. Lila, a small-time actress with little recent experience in domesticity enjoys temporarily keeping house. The festivity of the occasion has heightened her spirits; she and Kenny dance to radio music. Lila pretends that they are young lovers, but she apparently does so in all innocence. However, Kenny finally gives way to the desire which has been growing in him during the last month; and he begins to kiss Lila passionately.

When Helen comes home, she is somewhat tense and obviously suspicious. She notes that Kenny and Lila have been drinking together, and she also discovers that they have been dancing. This intimacy makes her uneasy, but she controls herself well. However, Kenny's giving her the watch which he has bought, is more than she can stand, and acts dramatically as a triggering device. Helen says that she cannot accept the gift, and this rejection leads to Kenny's declaration that he is going to leave home. Lila's dinner is left untouched as Kenny stamps out. The watch symbol comes to its full realization just before Lila leaves the Baird household. Kenny, who has now made love to Lila, gives her the watch, clearly indicating that his attempt to replace his father in his mother's life has now been abandoned and that he has through Lila found the solution to his complicated problem. But what Inge intends to suggest is not credible in reality; the solution is just too pat and too suddenly arrived at.

Lila is the play's most compelling character, and her psychological development is essentially quite authentic and believable although often too obvious to have dramatic impact. Her beginnings are obscure, although the audience is told that her mother lived until the time of Lila's unfortunate marriage and subsequent suicide attempt. Lila's one statement about her mother provides an interesting parallel to Kenny's feelings about his: "I guess Mama wondered about a lotta things in my life. I'm kinda relieved she's dead now. I don't feel I have to account to anyone any more" (47-48). This statement, of course, is pure rationalization. What Lila is saying essentially is that nobody cares about her; she is a free agent, but she doesn't really wish to be. This point is broached later in the play when Lila's lover, Ricky, is about to arrive; and Helen suggests that the two might want to spend the night together. Helen appears to be a broad-minded, understanding friend when she makes her suggestion to Lila; but she is really eager to get Lila out of the house since she herself must work all night and since she does not at this point trust Lila to be alone all night with Kenny, who might return. She tells Lila: "I'm not a prude. . . . I may be religious but I'm not a prude. I know your life has been different from mine. A beautiful girl like you, out with a show. I knew Ricky was your lover the minute I saw him. I don't sit in judgment on people" (83). Lila tells Helen that she is wonderful; but one is not convinced that Lila believes this. As Lila is portrayed, she needs someone to tell her the rules of the game and to force her to obey them; she is painfully aware that no one really cares enough about her to set up any prohibitions against her promiscuous behavior.

Lila acknowledges that she is emotionally immature and con-fides to Helen that "sometimes I feel like a child, just as helpless as a child, and as afraid as a child. And when I get afraid, that's when I do silly things. When I'm afraid, I want somebody close to me, Helen. I don't care who it is" (85). She concludes this speech by admitting that sometimes she hates herself. Lila's basic insecurity is further increased when Helen takes no moral stand against her affair with Ricky. Yet Inge cannot permit Helen to take a moral stand, for her doing so would weaken his presentation of Lila as surrogate mother and would emphasize Helen's maternal interest in her. The more nearly Inge can present Helen and Lila as equals, the more control does he have over the development of the Oedipus theme in the play.

One may wonder why Lila enters the play as she does with a band of characters who are not necessary to the development of the plot. To begin with, these characters show Lila in the milieu which she is leaving. They represent a much more sophisticated world than Lila will find in small-town Kansas with Helen and Kenny. It is also well for Inge to have Lila arrive with this group in tow because the first scene of the play, a dinner scene between Helen and Kenny, certainly is, as Gerald Weales has written, "one of the dullest passages in the Inge canon,"[3] and the need for immediate contrast is obvious. The contrast, however, is not provided very forcefully by Madame Olga, a lusty but somewhat hackneyed grandame; by Ronny, a somewhat prototypical homosexual who has been playing juvenile roles for twenty years and whose libido is on occasion put down by Madame Olga's stern authority; and by Ricky, a wholly wooden character who plays "heavies" and who is Lila's lover and unofficial manager. Weales is correct in his feeling that "what the play needs at this point . . . is some big, boozy theatrical caricatures that might wake up the play."[4] Although Inge's basic idea of introducing Lila's friends is good, it is lost in rather pedestrian dialogue, quite devoid of the sort of wit to which the basic situation would have lent itself. As they are presented, these supernumeraries temporarily block the play's development. As the play stands, the only function which these characters serve is that they leave Lila behind them in a void. But Inge does not capitalize on Lila's loneliness when she is left at the Bairds. Indeed, she plunges rather volubly into conversation with Helen, and they relive together parts of their common past. There is little indication that Lila is any lonelier here than she would be anywhere else. Because she is adrift, Lila has a certain inherent loneliness, but this is so fundamental a part of her that geographical location has little to do with it. Her loneliness is psychological; personal isolation is something she has learned to live with.

Lila's personal isolation is often illustrated throughout the play, but never so clearly as when Helen suggests that Lila try to make friends outside the Baird household and asks her, "Why don't you call on Mrs. Mulvaney sometime? She's about your age and I know you'd like her." But Lila resists this suggestion: "I'm awful shy about meeting new people, Helen. Nice married women like her, who have kids and go to church and seem so

happy . . . I just don't seem to have anything in common with"
(74). The play gives no evidence that Lila has ever really tried
to establish any common ground between herself and other
people. It is her permanent sense of loneliness which motivates
her affair with Kenny and which makes her almost plead with him
to marry her afterward—her actual spoken words never contain
the plea; her tone of voice is the key to her pleading.

Lila is never in control of her own destiny, as the ending of
A Loss of Roses makes clear. Ricky is himself desperate, but
only because of his bad luck; he finds physical gratification in
Lila, nothing more. Marriage is definitely not a part of his overall plan, as Lila well knows. Ricky, although never anything but
a flat character in Inge's play, is thoroughly unscrupulous and
disreputable. He finds Lila a job in movies; and, after building
up her hopes, he reveals that he has arranged for her to act in
"blue movies" and to do a degrading night-club act as well.
When Lila refuses, he threatens to blackmail her and also em-
ploys physical abuse to get her to accede to his scheme. Kenny
reappears on the scene, almost melodramatically; and Ricky is
sent off. But after her affair with Kenny and after a half-hearted
suicide attempt, Lila realizes that her only real solution is to do
what Ricky has proposed. She has him come and take her away
to Kansas City to an unsavory and uncertain future.

Inge has realized since the Broadway production of A Loss of
Roses that he should have concentrated the ending of his play on
Lila's departure in order to focus attention more upon her than
upon Helen and Kenny. The anticlimax runs its course when
Ricky arrives to take Lila away. However, the author unfortunately divides attention in the last scene and insists upon
stating what he has already clearly implied—that Kenny has
freed himself and will leave home. The introduction of Mrs.
Mulvaney and her small daughter in the last minutes—indeed,
in the last seconds of the play—is clumsy and unwarranted.
Sandra Mulvaney represents the young innocent. The sight
of the little girl on her way to the first day of school
launches Lila on the most unfortunate bit of dialogue in the
play. She recounts her story of taking roses to her teacher on
the first day of school and of how she ended up being slapped
and scolded by the teacher (the title of the play is derived from

this speech in which roses and innocence are equated). However, if Inge is trying to suggest here that the theme of the play is the loss of innocence, he is misleading his audience. Innocence has been lost when the play begins. The theme of the play is that there is great depression in the human condition and that there is little means of ameliorating it. One just learns to live with it, making what compromises he must in order to continue an existence which is never demonstrably worth-while.

Inge's attempt to free Kenny from his strong tie to his mother is a central issue in the play. Every indication is given that Kenny does not want to leave home. He prefers to be a filling-station attendant and to live with his mother rather than to take a much better position which has been offered him in Wichita. Although he has much surface conflict with his mother, Kenny also has very strong emotional ties to her. He has very little respect for any women aside from his mother. He shuns the attempts of any socially acceptable girls to get to know him, but dates the sort of girl he can pick up at the skating rink. When Jelly Beamis accuses Kenny of "getting his kicks" and then of finding out that he hasn't any money to treat his dates, Kenny tells him: "I'm not wastin' any money on the bags we pick up" (16). Jelly says to him, "You never take anyone to the movies but your old lady," and Kenny replies that he doesn't "put any of the bags we pick up in the same class with my mom." His feelings are revealed later in the play when he tells Lila: "I always wanted to do something for Mom. I mean . . . I've always felt like I owed her something. . . . she coulda got married again, if it hadn't been for me. . . . I feel sorry for her now, without a husband to do things for her" (62). He continues, "I think a lot of Mom. I guess I don't always show it" (63); and then he states his feelings in a dialogue that has the familiar tone of a *Reader's Digest* essay on motherhood.

Inge chooses to drive home the point of Kenny's liberation by having Kenny tell Lila of his troubled dream during their night of love. "I . . . I dreamed that someone died," he tells Lila. "It was . . . Mom. . . . She had to die, for some reason. She had to. It was terrible" (98). Unfortunately, this dream can very reasonably be interpreted to mean, "I have killed Mom," in which case Kenny's decision to leave home becomes inconsistent. For, in waking and finding the dream untrue, the guilt suggested by the dream would be assuaged; and the relief which would ensue might reasonably keep Kenny in his trap rather than free him. This dream is much less valid in its implications than were Lola's dreams in *Come Back, Little Sheba;* they serve to explain her conflicts and to give a clear indication of the only reasonable resolution of these conflicts. Kenny's dream serves no such purpose and can only churn already muddied waters.

Inge's characters are usually caught up in a rather zestless existence. The settings of his plays promote this effect, which is also promoted by the zestless responses of the characters in a number of instances. Kenny is often characterized by his almost defeated answers that things are "OK." In *Come Back, Little Sheba,* Lola often responds to occurrences with an almost identical lack of enthusiasm, with the usual response, "That's nice." This sort of lacklustre reply is an indication of the spiritual bankruptcy which Inge's characters often represent. They withdraw emotionally into an anesthetic state which is their only protection from pain.

In *A Loss of Roses,* Inge plays vaguely with various sex themes. He develops the Oedipus theme rather fully; however, he also hints at the homosexual theme by introducing Ronny into the play; he has Lila tell of her peculiar relationship to her husband, Ed Comiskey, whose father, posing as Ed's brother, tries repeatedly to seduce her; he implies a fundamental sadism in the Lila-Ricky affair; and he very clearly indicates the sexual overtones which are present in Kenny's kleptomania—Kenny steals only valueless objects (gloves, an empty change purse), but always from women. Helen Baird's reaction to hearing about the sexually complicated lives of the people in the tent show in which Lila played during her marriage to Ed Comiskey is a clue to some of her own fears: "Oh, that's shocking. . . . I've never heard of such people. . . . you should have reported that Mr. Comiskey to the police. The man was a degenerate" (45). What Helen is really saying is not that she hasn't heard of such people but that she prefers to turn her back on the reality of their existence, just as she prefers not to acknowledge on any conscious level the real problem in her own life. Helen can be described accurately as a strong woman; but her strength has been built up arduously and a concomitant of it is a rigid personality. Beneath all of her strength is a pervasive insecurity.

A Loss of Roses is often lacking in inner motivation. Much of the action is lost, at least partially, in talk—and the talk is not always convincing. There are other false notes in the play which serve to weaken its dramatic credibility.[5] The amateurishness of a great deal of the psychological presentation is often downright misleading. *A Loss of Roses* is the first Inge play in which the characters are used primarily for the purpose of presenting plot. Generally the author has permitted characterization to dominate, the plot and theme being natural outgrowths of the characterization. But in this play Inge appears to have begun with plot; the characters are servants to the plot, and the theme is permitted to develop as it will.

Perhaps Inge's greatest difficulty in this play is that he is concerned with two basic stories: the Helen-Kenny story and the Lila story. He never really succeeds in welding the two stories with such deftness that the seam does not show.

II   Splendor in the Grass*

Splendor in the Grass is a warm and understanding psychological study of two adolescents who are deeply and passionately in love but who must control and restrain this love until the boy is ready to enter the world of business which his ambitious father envisions for the reluctant lad. The story is set in eastern Kansas, and the bulk of the action takes place before the stock market break of 1929. A few anticlimactic scenes occur after this event, and the final scene takes place presumably in 1933 or 1934. The period covered, then, takes the audience from the peak of prosperity, which the discovery of oil in Kansas and Oklahoma heralded, to the period of the dust bowls in the same area. The economic events of the period are roughly parallel to the emotional situations of the two principals in the film, Bud Stamper and Wilma Dean Loomis, generally referred to as "Deanie."

*All references to *Splendor in the Grass* will be to the Bantam Book Edition (# J2204) of the scenario, which was published in 1961.

Bud is the only son of Ace Stamper, a self-made man whose oil company is experiencing unequaled success. As the film opens, a new gusher has just come in, and Stamper stock has risen fourteen points in a day. But Ace, not at all atypically, is an unhappy man. His only daughter is a nymphomaniac who causes him no end of pain; but he is more pained about what people will say and think than he is at the desperation of his daughter's situation. Mrs. Stamper is a wooden character in the film, but the little one does see of her suggests the protagonist in Evan Connell's *Mrs. Bridge*. Bud is his father's one hope for the future; for, as Ace idealizes him, he represents all that is meaningful in life. He is strong, he is the star player on the high school football squad, and he seems amply endowed to continue on the course which his father is now charting in the oil business. Ace dreams that Bud will go to Yale and will then become an executive at Stamper Oil.

But all that Bud really wants in life is to study agriculture at the state "cow college" and to run his father's ranch. Bud is eager to marry Deanie, and he dreams of doing so before he goes to school so that she will be able to accompany him. Obviously, this plan would not coincide with Ace's plans to send his son to Yale; but Deanie could go off to agricultural college with Bud.

Deanie is a sweet, genuine girl. Bud is her whole life, and she can conceive of no future which does not include him. Nevertheless, she is willing to wait for him to finish Yale if, in the course of events, he must go there. Deanie's father, a small-town grocer, is a sympathetic and sensitive man. Her mother is a garrulous, somewhat domineering woman; but she, too, is basically a sympathetic type. Presumably Deanie is the only child of Del Loomis and his wife. Del is experiencing his first limited taste of prosperity as the film opens because he has bought some Stamper Oil Company stock which is now growing in value with whirlwind speed.

The economic gap between Bud and Deanie is substantial, but the cultural gap is hardly noticeable since both come from basically simple small-town families, one of which is newly rich and the other modestly comfortable. Inge might have chosen to turn his scenario into a Montague-Capulet type of conflict, in which case the plot would have been contrived and completely predictable. However, Ace Stamper is no Montague; he is too realistic to fight directly the love situation between Bud and Deanie. He never forbids Bud's marriage to Deanie; indeed, he goes so far as to admit to his son: "She's a nice kid. (And a looker!)" (8). But he tells Bud: "all I'm asking is that you finish Yale and then if you still wanna marry the li'l Loomis girl, I'll give you both my blessing and send you off to Europe on a honeymoon. But please wait, Bud" (29). Ace is, beyond anything else, the realist. He realizes that to forbid the marriage would be to force it and that to delay it will be to destroy any chance of its taking place. He further leads to the destruction of the pure and happy relationship which Bud and Deanie have achieved by telling his seventeen-year-old son, in a moment of fatherly cameraderie and understanding, "Son, what you need for the time being is another kind of girl. Yes. When I was a boy, there was always two kinds a girls. And we boys never mentioned them in the same breath. But once in a while, one of us boys'd sneak off with one of the girls that . . . well . . . get a little steam outa our system" (29). Ace, a crass, insensitive businessman type, cannot understand that his son is trying to be an idealist—or, if he understands this, he equates the quality with weakness and tries to direct his son toward a more realistic view of life. And Bud, although he is not shown to have any overwhelming respect for his father, is necessarily influenced by his father's advice which inevitably affects his relationship with Deanie.

Ace's dealings with Bud are hardly admirable. He plays upon the boy's sympathy and elicits from Bud the sort of behavior which he wishes by making Bud feel that he controls Ace's happiness. Ace is very much aware of the fact that he is a self-made man, and he drives this point home to Bud at every opportunity—"I wasn't much older than you, Bud, when I fell off that crown block and hit the rig floor. And my running days were long gone. So you're running for both of us now" (8). When Ace speaks of his daughter, he tells Bud, "God knows, I've had one disappointment already . . . I've got all my hopes pinned on you now, Son!!!" (9-10). And when Bud broaches the question of his marrying Deanie and going to agricultural college, Ace does not rant and rave, but very effectively and tragically says, "I can't stand another disappointment, Son" (29). Ace's statement is utter tripe; he would adjust to Bud's marriage in two weeks, and as a grandfather he would be obnoxiously boastful. But he uses the most selfish sort of tactics to direct and to control his son's life.

Although Ace is not a leading character, he is the film's most important secondary character; and Inge's portrayal of him is masterful throughout the scenario, the more so because Ace fits so naturally into a stereotype. However, Inge never loses a chance to develop his portrayal of Ace further, and he succeeds in creating a character which is far more than a mere stereotype. Ace is a totally materialistic person. He cannot understand that his son and Deanie are in love, for he has probably never been capable of love himself; a number of his statements indicate that to him love is synonymous with sex. And Ace knows full well that sex can be bought.

But Ace also thinks that everything and everyone has a price. When Bud is ill with pneumonia and it seems possible that he might not recover, Ace encounters Doc Smiley in the hospital and tells him, "If you pull this boy through there's a bonus waiting for you. A big one. Five thousand dollars. Five thousand" (53). This statement is indicative of Ace's standards; he can be and has been bought—and he can buy.

Ace has no real grounds for not wishing Bud to marry Deanie —except that, at this time in America's social development, it was not usual for married men to attend college as full-time students. However, there was no financial barrier to Bud's marriage; and, although the play never states it, Ace probably objects because he thinks Bud will soon be able to make a better marriage.

One might have expected Ace to reconsider Bud's marriage to Deanie after Bud has nearly succumbed to pneumonia; but Ace again thinks that money can cure any wounds of the heart, and when Bud leaves the hospital, he gives him a new car rather than a new way of life. Inge uses this new car to precipitate Bud's affair with Juanita which, of course, leads to the breakdown of his romance with Deanie.

Ace is the realist about everything but Bud, for obviously Ace is living vicariously through Bud the youth of which he was deprived. Ace tries to foist upon Bud all that he thinks he would have wanted as a youth; but Ace is actually trying to shape Bud to the socially approved mold and nothing more. Yale is a fundamental part of this mold, and Ace is desperate when it becomes clear to him that Bud is not going to succeed at Yale.

Ace's suicide is amply prepared for and is convincing. Throughout the film, Ace has two basic motivations—his continued material success and his sanguine expectations for Bud. He loses both of these motivating factors simultaneously; and, having interfered irrevocably with Bud's life, he does the only thing left for him to do—he plunges from the hotel window to dash himself to death on the pavement below. But his action is impetuous. On the night of his suicide he takes Bud to Tex Guinan's in New York where Tex, in the floorshow, makes light of the very thing which Ace is to do: "Tonight as I was walking along Park Avenue to get a taxi, I had to dodge the bodies jumping out of the windows" (101). Ace, who has drunk too much, says to Bud, "You see, Bud, I'm not gonna be around much more," but he hastens to add quite convincingly, "Oh, now, don't sound so worried, Son, I got no plans a kickin' off for a while" (102). But within a short time Ace is dictating a suicide note to the prostitute he has brought back to his hotel from Tex's club and minutes later he is dead.

Ace's death marks the end of Bud's career at Yale—one about to end anyway. But now the Stamper family is bankrupt; and Bud, managing somehow to save his father's ranch from the creditors, returns there to live the life which he had wanted for himself in the first place, but with a major difference. Now he cannot have Deanie because she is in a mental institution; instead, he marries an Italian girl, Angelina, of whom his father would have approved much less than of Deanie.

Bud bears certain broad resemblances to Biff in *Death of a Salesman*, and this film might indeed have been entitled *Death of a Man*, for Ace dies by his own hand; and Bud, the appealing young athlete, is ground out of existence only to become by the end of the play precisely the kind of man that Deanie describes when she says that he is "like other men all over the world, trying to get along" (120). The idealized Bud is dead.

Left to his own devices, Bud was a remarkably uncomplicated

character. He was not overly strong, but he was devoted and dutiful both as Deanie's fiancé and as Ace's son. When his duty to his father came into conflict with his duty to Deanie, Bud could not resolve the issue, and Deanie lost by default more than by Bud's plan. Inge might have done more to show the extent of some of Bud's conflicts. He does to some extent early in the play when he has Bud go down the hall of the high school slamming the locker doors and creating a great deal of noise. The direction accompanying this action tells the reader of the scenario that "Bud's a mystery to himself. He has no idea why there is so much violence in him lately" (16). Again when Bud is playing football, he tackles an opponent with what Inge describes as "a crushing blow." The directions continue, "An official charges up furiously, pointing at Bud as if murder has been committed" and calls, "This side penalized . . . fifteen yards. UNNECESSARY ROUGHNESS!!!" (19). The climax of the film would have been better realized had there been more instances of this sort of behavior on Bud's part.

Inge's understanding and recording of adolescent behavior is nothing short of amazing. The small touches which were almost entirely lacking in *A Loss of Roses* are present with vigor in *Splendor in the Grass*. The great irony of the story is that Deanie and Bud are living in strict accordance to the conventional codes of morality—even though to do so is almost impossibly difficult for them—but the adults toward whom they look for understanding are either ineffectual in helping them to solve their problems or are openly suspicious of their relationship. When Bud virtually pleads with Doc Smiley to give him some sort of guidance in solving his problem, all Doc can say is, "Bud, it's hard to advise you," and then he says, "Well, come in Friday and I'll give you some more vitamins and a sun-lamp treatment" (55); with this statement the doctor escapes the dilemma.

Deanie faces a problem with her mother who asks her if she and Bud have "gone too far already?" Deanie assures her mother that they haven't, but asks her mother what is in her heart: "Mom . . . is it so terrible to have those feelings about a boy?" Her mother replies that "no nice girl does," and goes on to propound the hypocritical philosophy which Inge has always been concerned with exposing: "Your father never laid a hand on me until we were married! And then I just give in because a wife has to. A woman doesn't enjoy those things like a man does" (p. 4). In essence, Mrs. Loomis, who is undoubtedly well meaning, makes her daughter feel that her emotions toward Bud set her apart, make her some sort of social pariah.

The scene fades and shortly shifts to the Stamper home which is in sharp contrast to the small Loomis house. Bud faces the same sort of interrogation from his father that Deanie has had from her mother. Ace says finally, "You're not goin' to do anything you'll be sorry for, are ya?" (8). Both Deanie and Bud are humiliated even though they have borne the pain of unfulfilled passion and have fought to retain the standards which their families so fumblingly attempt to uphold.

Inge is also skillful in his presentation of the high school scenes which he introduces into the film. He gives evidence of understanding the types of people, both adolescent and adult, that one finds in a high school—the teacher whose own sexual frustration makes her jealous of any signs that her students have found fulfillment; the girl students who hold in awesome esteem a girl who, like Deanie, has found the elation of complete identification with another human; the slithering, insecure, over-sexed Juanita; the boy, Toots, who doesn't know what love is but who has a keen sexual awareness and has found in the Juanita type of girl an easy means of satisfaction. The whispering in the back of the classroom is as authentically represented as it possibly can be; Inge has caught the exact cadences of these clandestine conversations and has made them contrapuntal to the classroom recitation which is going on simultaneously.

The river becomes a point of reference in the scenario and is used with good dramatic and artistic effect. The action opens with a passionate love scene between Bud and Deanie who are in Bud's car beside the river. This part of the local lovers' lane is specifically their territory, a fact made clear when Bud brings Juanita to the same place but, realizing where he is, suggests that they go to another place. At the river, also, Bud makes his declaration to Toots that Deanie is now fair game—Toots declares that, since Bud is no longer dating Deanie, this is his chance. He then says to Bud, "Any objections?"; and Bud answers, "I can't stop you" (62). The answer is clearly one of defeat—essentially Bud's attitude throughout the remainder of this portion of the film.

The river is especially significant in the development of the story because the film's climactic scene, Deanie's attempted suicide, takes place here. Toots has taken her to the spring prom where she sees Bud for the first time in several weeks. Determined to end the suffering and uncertainty which she has been going through by offering herself to Bud, she goes out to the parking lot with him. Inside the car, Deanie cries, "Take me Bud. Take me. Here. Right here. I don't care. . . . I'll do anything, Bud. . . . I haven't had a happy moment since you stopped seeing me. . . . I want to stay here with *you*. I want *you*" (75-76). Bud, who cannot put Deanie in a class with Juanita or with his nymphomaniac sister, rejects her advances. This rejection is more than Deanie can bear; so she bolts from the car, runs away, and plunges into the river. This act confirms her father's opinion that she should be placed under a doctor's care in a psychiatric hospital in Wichita, to which Deanie is sent to be treated while Bud goes to Yale, each having been forced to yield to the forces which would separate them. In the hospital Deanie is to meet the man she will marry just to keep from being alone; and in New Haven Bud meets Angelina, the understanding waitress, whom he is to marry.

When Bud stops seeing her, Deanie is in a more unhappy situation than Bud, who can at least look forward to some hopeful future—he will go on to college and, as far as he knows, will one day be in command of his father's rising business. Inge says nothing of Deanie's future; he leaves this point vague because Deanie's future without Bud *is* vague and this fact makes her the more appealing to the audience. It also makes her suicide attempt more convincing.

It is ironic that Ace's comment to Bud after Deanie's suicide attempt is, "I told you she wasn't for you. You wouldn't wanta be chained the rest of your life to a girl who was . . . unstable" (84), and that Ace later commits suicide. The two basic values which are in conflict throughout the film are emphasized by the suicide attempt and by the accomplished suicide: Deanie, an idealist, tries to end her life because of love; Ace, a materialist, ends his life because he cannot face his inevitable financial failure. And to Ace, his reason for suicide is the only justifiable one. He never comes to understand the force of love, and this is his tragedy. Even his feeling for his son is one of possession, not love.

If *A Loss of Roses* was condemned by a number of critics because it talked itself to death, a similar condemnation of *Splendor in the Grass* would certainly not be valid. In writing of *The Dark at the Top of the Stairs,* Harold Clurman said that Inge "writes sparsely, almost laconically, but his choice of words and of situations is so shrewd that he makes them go a long way in creating a stage life far more potent than the written page may indicate."[6] One might make precisely the same observations about *Splendor in the Grass.* Inge constantly draws the rein tight on his dialogue and presents the content of the play with sensitivity and subtlety. Whereas, in *A Loss of Roses* he very clumsily supplies background information by having the principals give to each other information which they obviously would already be expected to know, when he needs to provide similar information in his scenario, he does it by having the characters talk almost to themselves, to muse about the past. An example of this is found in Ace's speech (8) already quoted earlier in another connection, which begins "I wasn't much older than you."

Inge is never guilty of overwriting in this work, as he sometimes was in *A Loss of Roses.* In his scenario he has returned to the crisp dialogue of *Picnic* and of *Bus Stop.* He treats his situations deftly and prefers to suggest them rather than to elaborate on them. One might note, for example, the economy of the two hospital scenes: the first, when Bud is ill with pneumonia; the second, when Deanie has attempted suicide. The first is used primarily to show that Ace thinks he can buy anything including the life of his gravely sick boy. Inge achieves the impression in seven very clipped speeches between Doc Smiley and Ace, after which he shifts the scene to the church where Deanie is praying for Bud's recovery. This shift, which emphasizes the difference between Ace and Deanie, sketches more deeply the impression which Inge wishes the audience to form of each. The author tells the audience nothing; rather he has the characters demonstrate through their actions what each represents. The long speeches of *A Loss of Roses* are replaced by clipped dialogue and cogent interaction of characters.

The second hospital scene is somewhat longer, but serves a manifold purpose. First, it shows the differing attitudes of Mr. and Mrs. Loomis toward Bud. Secondly, it really marks the climax of the play—the climax begins actually with Deanie's decision to go to the dance and ends with the announcement that Deanie must go to a psychiatric hospital—for in this hospital scene Bud reaches his decision to buck his father and marry Deanie. He says, "I'm eighteen and that's legal age in this state. I'm going to marry her" (83). But Doc Smiley tells Bud that it will be a number of years before Deanie is ready to marry; and here, dramatically at least, the movie ends. Circumstance has now forced the decision toward which the film has been working, and everything that follows is anticlimactic and dramatically unnecessary.

One might reasonably ask whether Inge did not make too great a compromise in continuing the play beyond the second hospital scene. It is highly unlikely that he would have written beyond this scene had he been presenting it to a Broadway audience. However, the larger and less sophisticated audience to which most films are geared is concerned with outcomes, and Inge had to recognize this fact and give obeisance to it. He succeeds in building toward a second climax in the final meeting between Bud and Deanie; in this scene is the conventional Hollywood ending which is quite different from Inge's endings up to this point. Nothing is solved by sex at the end of *Splendor in the Grass* as it is in some of the author's earlier plays; instead, everything is solved by the passage of time, by Deanie's recognition that Bud is very much like every other man. Had the film ended with the second hospital scene, the ending would have been essentially a romantic one; but, ending as it does, it moves from the romantic to a mildly pessimistic determinism, suggestive of the Naturalists. This ending is by no means a Thomas Hardy or a Frank Norris one—nor, indeed, is the ending of a play like *Streetcar Named Desire* naturalistic in the sense, for example, of the ending of *Tess of the D'Urbervilles* or *McTeague*—for it is not so decisive as an early Naturalist would have made it. However, this is Naturalism in a minor key. Death is not the ending here; rather, as in Inge's other dramas, the principals have both made the compromise which will enable them to go on living.

But usually the author has made the compromise a bit more palatable—especially in *Bus Stop* and in *The Dark at the Top of the Stairs*—by indicating that sex can overcome all difficulties. One does not have this feeling at the end of *Splendor in the Grass*. Bud and Angelina are eking out an existence and raising a family, but Bud will never know real love again. Even if he were to win Deanie again, he could not know the love for her which he once did. He has passed beyond that period in his life; he is a different person and so is she. Deanie will marry the young man whom she met at the psychiatric hospital; but she has experienced the one all-consuming love in her life, and she will never relive it.

In films, Inge was able to shift easily and gracefully from scene to scene. Such flexibility is generally impossible on Broadway even on a stage with revolving sections. In the film, Inge was able to touch on points briefly for illustration, and then leave them to move on to something else. The pace and forward thrust of his film story distinguish it from any of his other work. Despite the length of its anticlimax, *Splendor in the Grass* marks a new vigor in Inge's work. He has wedded poignance and understanding with effective dialogue and well-conceived characterization. His total result is promising and, in itself, highly effective.

III   Natural Affection*

Amazingly, *Natural Affection* closed after a very short run on Broadway; for, although the play is seriously defective, the most significant defects are concentrated toward the end of the play. It would, presumably, have been a simple job to cut the play halfway through the second act, reduce the extremely offensive sensationalism which begins when the Brinkmans come to Sue and Bernie's apartment on Christmas Eve, and bring about the resolution without Donnie's senseless murder of a stranger at

---

*References to *Natural Affection* are to the Random House edition of the play published in 1963.

the end of the play. Inge contends that he was writing of things as they really happen, just as one reads of lurid events in the newspaper every day: "There was one story I read of a boy who, rejected by his mother and sent back to a work farm, ran out onto the street and killed the first woman he saw for vengeance. In his heart, he could never admit how much he hated his mother. He had to kill a substitute" (ix). Any casebook in psychiatry records instances of this sort of senseless and brutal murder. However, drama remains an art form; and, as such it is, even in the realistic extremes, differentiated from newspaper reporting in that it selects and presents its material with some attention to artistic effects. The present play has attempted in its last quarter to replace real drama and genuine dramatic effect with sensationalism and vulgarity.

The artistic question which the play poses is, therefore, whether the playwright should resort to using these literary props in order to achieve an effect which can be achieved through other means. In writing of Odets' *Till the Day I Die*, Edith Isaacs objected to the author's showing a Gestapo officer smashing the hand of Ernst Tausig, a violinist. She wrote in *Theatre Arts Monthly* that she hoped Odets would "come to know . . . that an audience can feel longer and more deeply the pain in a violinist's mutilated hand if they see the effect of the hammer blow upon it instead of seeing the blow itself."[7] This statement is broadly applicable to *Natural Affection*. No one would suggest that an author not present truth; however, appropriate method is the question here. Inge, who had a strong play until he overemphasized the sensational elements, erred in being too direct and too literal.

The title of the play, *Natural Affection*, alludes to the affection which a mother feels for her son. In this case, the mother is Sue Barker, a rather beautiful woman described as being thirty-six years old, and the son is her illegitimate offspring, seventeen-year-old Donnie. Donnie, brought up in an orphanage, has never known the sort of affection which most young children experience. His mother has been devoted to him, but for many years she was not able to care for him because she had to work. The audience is told how she used to visit Donnie in the orphanage and how he used to cuddle up to her lovingly.

When she finally became successful as a buyer for a large department store, Sue was able to take Donnie to live with her; but he got into trouble and was sent to a work farm, a type of reform school. The play opens on the morning when Donnie is to return from this farm to spend his Christmas holiday with his mother. During Donnie's absence, Sue has moved into a luxurious apartment and has taken as her lover Bernie Slovenk, a Cadillac salesman some years her junior. As the play opens, Sue arises from the bed which she shares with Bernie and stands staring out the window. Bernie asks her what she is doing, and she replies—setting the mood for much of what is to follow— "Standin' here, lookin' out at the world. God, it looks ugly at times" (4). Inge claims to have used this line to prepare the audience for the ugliness which is to come in the play (Preface, vii). He also restates the line near the end of the play when Sue again stands looking out the window and says, "God, it's an ugly morning. Nothing out the window to look at but ugly, black buildings" (106). The play has about it the overall bleakness which these lines indicate.

The beginning of the play is brief and is concerned largely with Sue's reaction to Donnie's coming home and with her realization of the conflict which is likely to occur between her lover and her son. Bernie is uneasy about Donnie's arrival even though Sue tells him that the boy knows about their living together. But she tells Bernie, "Let's not have any love-making while he's here" (14).

The play's middle and the development of the central conflict begin with Donnie's arrival. No one is in the apartment when he arrives with Gil, a colleague from the work farm. Gil is brought on the scene temporarily just so that he and Donnie can engage in conversation which will reveal to the audience some of Donnie's problems at the work farm—he has had problems with a homosexual guard—and which will acquaint the audience with the fact that Donnie will not have to return to the farm if his mother agrees to keep him with her. But Bernie is the stumbling block; Sue needs Bernie sexually and it is evident that he is not about to marry her. Donnie needs Sue if he is to lead any sort of satisfactory existence, but his presence causes her relationship with Bernie to be strained. The resolution of the conflict comes when Sue reaches her decision after her sustained attempt to be the dutiful mother. She cries out at Donnie: "I'm not going to give up the rest of my life to keep a worthless kid I never wanted in the first place. Quit hanging on me, Donnie!" (144). As soon as she has uttered these harsh words, she tries to take them back; but the damage has been done. She goes offstage, and a drunken woman wanders in from the party next door looking for Bernie. Not finding him, she turns her attentions—and affections—to Donnie who reaches for a carving knife and stabs her to death.

The play has a strong Oedipus undertone, especially when Donnie first comes into the apartment and fondles his mother's clothing. Later, when Bernie leaves, Donnie, like Kenny in *A Loss of Roses,* tells his mother what a happy life they can have together: "I still love ya, Mom. Just as much as when I was a kid back in the orphanage. I still believed in God 'n' everything, and I used to pray we could be together. I thought you were the most wonderful woman in the world, and I wanted us to be together forever 'n' ever. . . . You got me, Mom. I can be just as much company as Bernie. (He tries to kiss her)" (112-13). The Oedipus situation in this play is heightened, however, by the fact that Sue is a virtual stranger to Donnie.

Natural Affection has a strong subplot in the relationship of Claire and Vince Brinkman, the couple who live in the apartment across from Sue and Bernie. Bernie has had an on-and-off affair with Claire; and, when he tires of her, he sends male friends of his to call. Claire, a vital and sensuous woman, is married to a wealthy, impotent man some years her senior. There is a strong suggestion—both Sue and Bernie mention it—that Vince has homosexual leanings and that these are directed toward Bernie. Vince, while not an alcoholic, drinks excessively and lives frenetically to block from his consciousness the hopelessness of his marriage to Claire. During his one drunk scene in the play, his dialogue is about as sexually frank as any dialogue which has come to the Broadway stage. The subplot presents a sharp contrast between the illicit love of Sue and Bernie, and the marriage relationship between Claire and Vince. It is clear in the final scene of the play that Bernie and

Sue really love each other but that Claire loathes Vince, who loves her very much.

Inge portrays Sue as a woman who has risen to a high position with her company because of her strong sense of responsibility and because she is naturally bright. She feels a deep responsibilty to Bernie, and it is heightened by the fact that he loses his job through a mischance on the day that Donnie returns home. Sue has also had a continued sense of her responsibility to Donnie. After she had conceived him out of wedlock and the man had run away, she did not have an abortion because "That kid was inside me, and I knew he was meant to *live*. I faced my responsibility, and it was the making of me. I've been strong ever since" (16). She calls Donnie's infancy "the happiest time in my whole life. . . . Even though I was so poor I couldn't buy him diapers, I was happy with him. And I felt proud" (18). Her feelings toward Donnie are strong—so strong, in fact, that they frighten and threaten her. Just as her responsibility to Bernie is heightened during the action of the play by the fact that he has lost his job, her responsibility to Donnie is increased by the knowledge of what he is suffering at the work farm. His back is scarred from a severe beating received from a sadistic guard: "This guard . . . he was a psycho . . . he got a *charge* from beating guys. Yah. Tha's the way he got his kicks" (42).

Bernie, a likable enough character, has neither Sue's native intelligence nor ability; however, he is in love with her and he is sincere in this love. He is rankled at making less money than Sue. He realizes that Donnie represents a threat to him, and he is resentful of the boy even before meeting him. Donnie is concerned about Bernie and wonders whether Bernie will like him. He discusses this problem with Sue, and she tries to reassure him. However, Inge places every conceivable obstacle in the way of Bernie and Donnie's getting along. Donnie, who arrives in old clothes and has to wear some of Bernie's clothes when he goes downtown to shop for new apparel, annoys Bernie by wearing his favorite cashmere jacket and his vicuña shirt. Because Bernie has wrecked a brand new Cadillac and lost his job at the Cadillac agency just before he meets Donnie, he arrives home feeling completely hopeless; and his irritation mounts as he discovers successively that Donnie has worn his clothing, has left the bathtub filthy, and is given to playing rock-and-roll records at full volume on the phonograph.

Donnie and Bernie are competing for the same woman, but their rivalry must be *sub rosa*. They are intensely jealous of each other; but Donnie has the upper hand because, first, he can say such things as "Doesn't Bernie ever pay for anything?" (71); secondly, because he catches Bernie kissing Claire passionately in the kitchen (86); and, thirdly, because Donnie has prior claim to Sue as her son. Try as they might, Donnie and Bernie cannot be friends, for the intensity of the competition between them is too great. Their rivalry must work upon Sue to force her into making a choice, and no choice can be satisfactory. She has to be the loser either way.

Donnie has gone through a difficult period of adjustment to life. He is at the work farm because he stole a car with some other boys and because he beat up a woman in Lincoln Park (12). Within the first few minutes of the play's action, Inge shows some of the manifestations of Donnie's aggressions, and he is so specific in presenting them that the audience has a foresight of what is to happen before the action of the play has run its course. Inge also deals specifically with Donnie's need for love. Sue tells Bernie: "He was shacking up with some old whore down on Division Street. She was buying him clothes. My Donnie! When he was fourteen years old. It just made me sick" (13). But all of this is deep in Donnie's past. He is presented on stage as a handsome, appealing, and sometimes touching youth. He is reaching out for love, and he is reaching out with unusual desperation because the alternative to winning his mother's genuine affection is returning to the work farm. Ruthless in competing with Bernie, he fights with any unfair weapon at his disposal. He tells tales on Bernie; and, in his last desperate bid for his mother's love, he tells her: "Bernie's no good. I told ya, he doublecrosses ya, and . . . He prob'ly wouldn't look twice at ya if you di'n' have all the money" (111). There is enough truth in what Donnie says to make Sue uncomfortable, and this sort of taunting causes her outburst which precipitates the play's final drastic action. Sue is a strong woman, but she is not sufficiently sure of herself and has not the inner security to be able to bear having Bernie's love for her questioned.

Donnie's desire to behave properly is used throughout the play to indicate how important it is to him to remain at home. In his first appearance with Gil, Donnie clearly states his desire to reform. He tells Gil, "I don't wanna do anything to get sent back to the cage" (30); and he obviously means this. Especially touching is Donnie's presentation to Sue of the Christmas gift which he has made her—a wooden *hors d'oeuvres* tray. He tells her, "I never gave anyone a Christmas present before, but I . . ."—and his voice trails off; then he says, thrusting the gift toward her, "Well, here" (77). When Sue is genuinely delighted by the gift, Donnie is almost unbelieving; he is also so overcome by emotion that he must leave the apartment so no one will see his tears. Donnie is irresistibly appealing here. His audience appeal is far greater than that of Kenny in *A Loss of Roses* or Sonny Flood in *The Dark at the Top of the Stairs* or any of a host of major Inge characters. His one limitation is that he is not entirely fair in his representation of Bernie to Sue; but this unfairness makes him the more appealing dramatically, for it gives the audience evidence of how desperately he needs love and of what measures he will take to secure it.

One might ask whether Donnie, as he is presented on stage, could reasonably commit the crime of violence with which the play ends. This crime is not Donnie's first evidence of violence against a woman. However, the crime for which he was sent away is merely told about remotely, and the Donnie who is presented to the audience is a reformed character. It is not impossible, however, that he would suddenly rebel as he did. He is a youngster who has suffered rejection through his life, and this rejection has just been stated and reiterated in positive terms by the distraught Sue. Donnie's act of violence is credible; but, as has been noted, it is dramatically an unsatisfactory ending for the play because the author depends upon shock effect and sensation for his conclusion. Artistically, the ending is tenable; dramatically and commercially, it was not. The audience reacted in such horror that the ending tended to blot out the rest of the play and to vitiate the earlier dramatic effects. Had the play ended with Donnie's kissing the woman passionately in the final act, the same end would have been achieved actually, and the audience reaction would have been much better. This would have been the same psychological turn used in *A Loss of Roses;* but, by ending the play with the beginning of a romance between Donnie and the woman, the author would have avoided the pitfalls which are evident in the ending of *A Loss of Roses.* The murder of the woman in *Natural Affection* is overt evidence of Donnie's severe reaction to being rejected by his mother; the seduction of this woman would have indicated the same basic reaction.

Vince Brinkman is the victim of rejection just as Donnie is, for Claire obviously does not love him. It is also apparent that she will never be satisfied with one man since she is basically immature, and she is so insecure that she needs the constant reassurance which she derives from the attentions of a wide variety of men. Vince is important to her because he fills the psychological need which none of her lovers can—he loves her worshipfully even though she rejects him. She feeds parasitically on this love and uses it to lessen her feelings of insecurity and loneliness. Although she loathes Vince and cannot love or respect him, this feeling does not lessen her need for him.

Vince loves to give people gifts. This is a form of overcompensation with him. He does not give Claire spending money, but he buys her lavish presents. He also lavishes gifts upon Sue and Bernie. In a sense he is trying to buy away his guilt which is a manifestation of such a complexity of causes that one could not possibly begin to enumerate them from the limited knowledge which one has of Vince through the play.

Claire is a child emotionally. She has not been used to having much economic security through her life. She constantly alludes to the fact that the Brinkman apartment is large, and uses this as a sort of status symbol. Claire was the baby of the family and she sometimes wishes she "was back home in Bloomfield with my Mommy and Daddy. But I just love Chicago. I wouldn't leave Chicago for anything in the world. I just wish I didn't get so lonely" (23). Claire and Vince merely intensify each other's loneliness.

Nearly every critic of *Natural Affection* has commented on the vulgarity and crudity of Vince's drunk scene. Vince raves on about sex almost to the point of embarrassment and the audience senses a marked degree of relief when he finally passes out. Inge has previously presented characters in other plays who are sexually unfulfilled and who are terribly preoccupied with sex— Lottie Lacey in *The Dark at the Top of the Stairs*, Rosemary in *Picnic*, and Jelly Beamis in *A Loss of Roses*. However, this play is the first by Inge in which Vince's type has been presented so drunk that he was on the verge of collapse. The vulgarity of his dialogue is not unconvincing, but the objection of critics was one of taste. Inge has countered the criticism by saying he felt he could create the atmosphere he was striving to achieve "only in writing of common people whose language is of the streets. I do not think I have written an immoral play. If others think so, I think it is *their* problem" (ix).

Despite the fact that the artist must be permitted freedom of expression, he must make, however, a decision in regard to how he will write. He can stick stubbornly to his literary guns and say, "The critics and the audience be damned." But the artist who takes this independent position must assume an attitude of indifference to commercial success and to popular acclaim. And because audiences simply refused to give Inge the ground which he demanded of them, *Natural Affection* was doomed. Inge was understandably disturbed by the commercial failure of this play in which he had considerable faith; it is altogether possible that he could have salvaged his effort by modifying the ending and by excluding or toning down Vince's drunk scene. The conscientious author does not like to be faced with the sort of decision which is suggested here; but Inge found himself in an either-or dilemma, and his rejection of the "either" left no question of how the dilemma would be resolved.

The writing in *Natural Affection* represents Inge's most successful sustained effort. Gone is the awkward presentation of background material which plagues his earlier plays. Background material is presented convincingly and in sufficient detail so that the audience follows the action easily and with the insights necessary for it to appreciate what is going on. Inge gracefully tells the audience that Donnie can stay at home permanently if his mother will have him; the audience knows this important fact long before Sue does. Donnie's history is related to Bernie very briefly on the morning of Donnie's arrival; it is natural that Sue should tell Bernie the things which she does, for he knows little more about the boy than does the audience. Donnie's arrival in the empty apartment with Gil provides the author with an additional opportunity to present background as naturally as possible.

Most of the speeches in the play are clipped, and the natural, free-flowing dialogue moves at a much better pace than it does in *Bus Stop, Come Back, Little Sheba,* or *The Dark at the Top of the Stairs* where rather boring fits of introspection overtook the main characters periodically and soliloquies resulted. In *Natural Affection* the dialogue is convincing, and the only fits of introspection—both Claire and Vince become introspective in the second act, and Sue becomes slightly introspective and reminiscent in the first act—pass quickly and are motivated by some specific cause such as Vince's drunkenness, Claire's extreme insecurity, or Sue's guilt at not having been able to give Donnie the attention which a mother usually gives children.

Inge chooses his setting well in the play. There is a dreariness in the climate and a forced gaiety in the season. There is also an irony in the presentation of the action during the Christmas holidays, but the season is useful to Inge in explaining why Donnie is home from school as well as in bringing about the crisis in the play. Sue's jealousy of Claire is partly attributable to the fact that Claire, taking advantage of the spirit of the season, has been quite free in kissing Bernie. Vince's intoxication in the early part of the evening is more convincing on Christmas Eve than it would be at some other time. The general sentiment of the mother-son relationship is made more poignant by the season.

Writing of the play in the New York *Times,* Howard Taubman comments on Inge's passage in *Natural Affection* in which Claire comments on Tennessee Williams' *Sweet Bird of Youth*: "I don't see how they let shows like that get by. I think something should be done about it. All the characters in it were *sick,* if you ask me. I don't see why we can't have plays about people who are respectable. I don't know where that Tennessee Williams *finds* the characters he writes about, do you?" (82). It is ironic that Claire, a Williams-like character, should be given this speech.

Taubman writes of the allusion to Williams: "One of Mr. Inge's characters, in an outburst of discontent with the world as it is, demands to know why Mr. Williams writes with such violence about such sick people. Before the play is finished, the joke becomes savagely ironic. For 'Natural Affection' . . . is about people whose emotional and psychic health is anything but certifiable." The irony of Claire's speech, of course, pervades the play. It heightens the idea that people are not able to see themselves in perspective, and it also prepares the way for Sue's ultimate decision, which results when her animal nature overcomes her human nature, that Donnie will have to return to the work farm.

It might appear to audiences that the play would have reached its resolution happily had Bernie gone along more with the spirit of the season and agreed to let Donnie stay with Sue and him. But this would have been a soap-opera ending at best; and it would also have been an utter impossibility for Donnie really wants his mother on his own terms. Donnie does nothing to make Bernie like him, even though he expresses apprehension about how Bernie will react to him.

In *Natural Affection,* Inge explores the nature of love, and each relationship in the play is concerned with this exploration. Sex is in some way a part of every love relationship in the play— including that between Donnie and Sue. Everyone in the drama is searching frantically for love, but the obstacles to it always seem greater than the emotion. When Vince comes home early on Christmas morning with some drunken people he has picked up, the woman who is hugging her young man directs him, "Tell me you love me, you sonovabitch, or I'm gonna get mad." He answers, "All right. I love you. Now, get the hell inside" (106). This blatantly insincere expression of love holds a trick mirror to all of the love shown in the entire play: love is a living arrangement and little more. Yet Sue cannot give up what she has with Bernie in order to save her son.

Natural Affection was well acted, and Kim Stanley's performance as Sue Barker was a striking one. The supporting cast, which included Harry Guardino as Bernie, Tom Bosley as Vince, Monica May as Claire, and Gregory Rozakis as Donnie, received vociferous acclaim. Tony Richardson was the director. Norman

Nadel of the New York *World-Telegram* began his appraisal of *Natural Affection*: "American playwright William Inge and English director Tony Richardson are a powerful new pair in the theater. For proof of this you need look no further than 'Natural Affection,' newly arrived at the Booth. The problem is that these two established artists don't know how to control that power." Nadel then accuses Inge and Richardson of being possessed of "eagerness to produce the dirtiest play of the year." Nadel claims that sex is the play's central theme and that "the exploration of several complex and troubled characters becomes only the accessory." The Broadway production gave this impression more than a reading of the play does, and the direction emphasized sexuality and made the crucial murder scene at the end a virtual sexual act. But one cannot be sure whether Inge intended that the interpretation be such. However, the frequent introduction of Donnie's twist record implies that a basic sexuality underlies much of the play, and it is somewhat notable that Donnie plays this record immediately after he has stabbed the woman.

Regarding the sensationalism of the play, Richard Watts wrote in the New York *Post* that apparently Inge "decided it was the qualities of sensationalism in the work of Williams and Albee that gave them their excellence and set out to beat them at their own game." But Watts concludes, justly and validly, that "the fact proved in 'Natural Affection' is that the sensationally lurid is not Mr. Inge's field. Instead of seeming an integral part of his work, it appears to be clumsily imposed, and, in the process of trying it, his splendid capacity for compassion and human understanding slowly disappear, and a kind of extravagant foolishness and ineptness is substituted."

Even though there is validity in this statement, one wonders why there was such objection to the sensationalism of this play when there was no notable objection to the same basic sort of sensationalism in *Splendor in the Grass*. Ace Stamper commits suicide in this play, Deanie lands in a mental institution, and prostitutes wander back and forth through the latter part of the action. However, it seems to be easier for an audience to take the shocks of sensationalism when it is introduced to them more gradually than it was in *Natural Affection*. The appearance of the woman on the scene, her attempted seduction of Donnie, and his murder of her are so unanticipated that they explode upon the spectator with the violence of a tornado. Like Doc's drunk scene in *Come Back, Little Sheba,* the murder scene becomes a sudden frenzy of activity; but in *Natural Affection,* the plays ends with the scene and the only resolution of the problem which the scene brings about is a horribly desolate one. The members of the audience have been made to identify with Donnie, and suddenly the rug is pulled from under them. They leave the theater in a state of shock.

Artistically, it does not seem possible to view *Natural Affection* as a failure; and its possibility of commercial success might be assured were relatively slight revisions made and were the direction undertaken by someone with the restraint, let us say, of Harold Clurman. This play is the first major production in which Inge has avoided the utter banality and drabness which one finds in the bulk of his characters in each full-length play after *Come Back, Little Sheba.*

IV *But in Their Stead, Curses*

Walter Kerr recently lamented the passing of the William Inge who had produced *The Dark at the Top of the Stairs* which Kerr called "a touching example of one of our commonest theatre experiences: the memory play." He points out that, "If Mr. Inge's mood had most often been rueful, it had always been warm. If the voices overheard in parlors and bars had always had a commonplace twang to them, their very commonness and familiarity had helped to stir our affection." But he complains that *A Loss of Roses* was "neither familiar in spirit nor touching in effect," and he goes on to blame this not on the playwright's momentary fatigue, but on a tendency in American theater for "the dramatist to work in an ever narrower range, and with an ever softer and more indulgent touch."[8] However, what Kerr says here is nothing new. The critics have objected through the years to Inge's narrow range, to his concentration on the same basic type of characters in all of his plays; and his range seems no narrower in *A Loss of Roses* than it was in his earlier plays. What is surprising is that, when Inge tried to broaden his range in *Natural Affection,* audiences and critics so strenuously objected.

A Loss of Roses was demonstrably weak in its misdirected focus. This problem was noted by several critics, chief among them Harold Clurman.[9] However, *Natural Affection* is not so demonstrably weak as *A Loss of Roses;* it has significant strengths which none of Inge's major productions before it had possessed. Much of the criticism of *Natural Affection* was based upon moral rather than dramatic considerations; such judgments of Naturalistic or Realistic literature are patently unjust. Verisimilitude is the prime necessity of such literature, and the achievement of it may well involve the use of language and actions offensive to audiences and reviewers. Especially unjust is the criticism which states that "the real weakness of the play [is] the application of extreme realism to a group of people profoundly unreal."[10] This unsupported statement just is not true, for the principals of the main plot and of the subplot are well conceived and have excellent psychological motivation as the discussion of this play demonstrates. Each character is well developed in terms of both his background and his reaction to the immediate situation in which the audience finds him. The characters are not always easy to accept, and they are not always pleasing as human beings; but in *Natural Affection* Inge creates convincing individuals. In his preface to the play he has written, "If my play is too bold for [audiences], I can understand their sensibility in not wanting to watch it. I have a similar sensibility. It was a very difficult play for me to write" (ix). In this statement appears the crux of much of the adverse criticism which the play has received.

John McCarten's suggestion that Inge was trying to "set himself up as a junior-varsity Tennessee Williams"[11] is not very flattering to Inge; however, there is probably an element of truth in this statement; for Williams' sensationalism—which Williams generally handles with aplomb—appears to have provided motivation for Inge's attempt to be sensational in his play.

Splendor in the Grass is not "slick" in the Hollywood sense of the term; however, the scenario has great fluidity and the medium for which Inge was writing permitted him to experiment with a broader approach to his work than had hitherto been possible for him. This scenario does not demonstrate the writing skill of *Natural Affection*. The latter, even with its present ending, has the makings of a fine film.

Splendor in the Grass would be a stronger film play if the conclusion followed more closely upon the climax. The wrap-up scenes employ the Dickensian device of showing how the story worked out in the end; this method seems contrived and unnecessary in modern drama, even in modern film drama. Ace Stamper's suicide should mark the dramatic end of the film.

What do the three works considered in this chapter indicate about the development of William Inge? Certainly the scenario indicates that the author might have a substantial future in original film writing. However, *Natural Affection* leads one to hope that Inge will continue in legitimate theater. *A Loss of Roses* is not without possibilities, but its success depends upon the author's making Lila the center of the action. This change would enable him to make the Oedipus problem less important, and much would be gained if this problem were stated less directly.

Perhaps it will take audiences a while to adjust to the fact that in *Natural Affection* Inge has changed his locale. The play is set in Chicago rather than in Kansas or Oklahoma, and Chicago is not important to the play. Any other large city would have served Inge's purposes as well. It seems unfortunate that those who had tired of Inge's former locale and former characters should react to his presentation of a new locale and new characters with the negation which was found in both the critical and popular reception of *Natural Affection*.

CHAPTER 4

Many a Voice of One Delight

> "All people are divided into two
> groups, those who participate and
> those who watch and observe."
> —From *The Strains of Triumph*

WILLIAM INGE has shown infinitely more variety in his one-act plays than in his full-length dramas. Part of this variety is apparent to one who examines the settings of these plays. Although the majority of his Broadway productions were set in Kansas or Oklahoma in the 1920's or 1930's, a number of the one-act plays are set in such locales as a mining town near Pittsburgh (*The Boy in the Basement*), New York (*To Bobolink, For Her Spirit* and *An Incident at The Standish Arms*), Southern California (*A Social Event*), and an unidentified seaside resort (*Memory of Summer* and *The Mall*). Three of the plays might have happened anywhere—*The Rainy Afternoon, The Strains of Triumph*, and *The Tiny Closet*—although the directions indicate that *The Tiny Closet* is set in a Midwestern city. *Bus Riley's Back in Town* is set in Texas, but a redaction of the play, *Glory in the Flower*, is set more nearly in Kansas or Oklahoma, although the directions do not specifically indicate this locale.

Variety of locale is hardly the chief characteristic which distinguishes the one-act plays from the longer plays. Taken as a group, the one-act plays deal largely with human frustration—as do the longer plays—but a large variety of classical psychological disorders is dealt with rather extensively in the shorter plays. *To Bobolink, For Her Spirit* and *A Social Event* deal essentially with extreme examples of the psychological phenomenon known as identification. *The Boy in the Basement* is concerned with homosexuality and has overtones of the Oedipus problem, as has *The Rainy Afternoon,* which is concerned, as well, with sadism. *The Tiny Closet* deals with repressed homosexuality, manifested in transvestism. *Memory of Summer* concentrates upon a woman faintly reminiscent of Blanche DuBois, in Williams' *A Streetcar Named Desire;* in this case, the woman, who shows some nymphomaniacal tendencies, cannot face simple realities (such as the fact that the ocean water is cold late in September), and tends both to hallucinate and to daydream to the point of being pathological. *Bus Riley's Back in Town* and *Glory in the Flower* both deal with the effect that the passage of time has upon two people who had a romance in their late teens and who meet again some years later; the final scenes of *Splendor in the Grass* are suggested by these plays. The Electra problem is mentioned briefly in *Bus Riley's Back in Town,* but this particular allusion is not carried over into *Glory of the Flower.*

The Mall treats the various faces of love—the young sailor and his seventeen-year-old girl; the middle-aged prostitute and the mentally unbalanced man who falls in love with her; the platonic relationship between the mentally unbalanced man and his friend who takes a purely paternal interest in his welfare, suggestive of the Virgil-Bo relationship in *Bus Stop;* the two respectable, middle-class housewives who represent dull, conventional, married existence, quite devoid of real love; and the two lecherous crones who are too old and ugly to find love, but who find vicarious pleasure in watching various lovers pass by the bench on which they sit chuckling obscenely and making undertone crude remarks.

The Strains of Triumph presents a love triangle broadly suggestive of the Marie-Turk-Bruce one in *Come Back, Little Sheba;* and into this situation is projected the sympathetic, older man who wants to be understanding and helpful but does not know how. *An Incident at The Standish Arms* has as its heroine a respectable matron who is deprived of married love through divorce and who has an affair which degrades her. The point of this play, however, is to show the hypocrisy of the conventional, socially acceptable person; and the love affair is used as a vehicle for presenting the play's basic theme more convincingly.

The person who is seriously interested in William Inge as a creative artist will profit immeasurably from studying his one-act plays, for many specific fragments from the one-act plays are used in the major plays. Inge, as has been seen, sometimes works a one-act play into a full-length play. Two of the shorter plays which will not be discussed in this chapter, inasmuch as they are discussed earlier, were bases for longer plays—*People in the Wind* for *Bus Stop; Farther Off From Heaven* for *The Dark at the Top of the Stairs*. Inge is now reworking *Bus Riley's Back in Town* into a full-length play and has considered expanding *The Boy in the Basement* similarly. Although he considers *The Mall* to be complete as it stands, there are in it the makings of a full-length production.

Some of the plays discussed here are little more than sketchy vignettes. Among these one must place *To Bobolink, For Her Spirit; Memory of Summer; The Rainy Afternoon;* and *An Incident at The Standish Arms. A Social Event* and *The Strains of Triumph,* although they are something more than mere sketches, are most fully realized as one-act plays. However, *People in the Wind, The Boy in the Basement, The Tiny Closet, Bus Riley's Back in Town,* and *Glory in the Flower,* are extremely well-realized works; they succeed well within the severe space limitations imposed by presenting them in one act.

All of these plays under consideration were written between 1949 and 1957. *Glory in the Flower,* the most recent of these plays, represents a merging of *Bus Riley's Back in Town* with elements from *The Boy in the Basement.* The earliest of the plays dealt with is *To Bobolink, For Her Spirit* which was written before Inge came to New York and while he was still teaching at Washington University in St. Louis.

In the one-act plays, one is especially aware of the intellectual influences that Tennessee Williams and Arthur Miller have exerted upon Inge. The Williams influence is by far the stronger and is seen in Inge's presentation of characters such as Viola in *Memory of Summer,* Bus Riley in *Bus Riley's Back in Town* and in *Glory in the Flower,* Mrs. Scranton in *The Boy in the Basement,* and Mr. Newbold in *The Tiny Closet.* The

Mall is mildly suggestive of the Williams of *Camino Real,* an atypical Williams production. Inge's dealing with the passage of time and with the implications of social change for the little man are suggestive of Miller. The salesman in *Bus Riley's Back in Town* and *Glory in the Flower*—who is reminiscent of Rubin Flood, incidentally—speaks in many respects like a Miller character: "There oughta be a law to keep things the way they are. Goll darn it, there oughta be a law" (*Glory,* 142).*

It is apparent to anyone reading the corpus of Inge's work that the author works with a somewhat standardized gallery of characters. The one-act plays add personalities to this gallery—Spencer Scranton and Mr. Newbold, for example—but anyone who has read Inge's major plays will continually come upon characters from them in the one-act plays. Sometimes the names are the same—Del Loomis, for example, is first mentioned in *Bus Riley's Back in Town* (although he does not appear on stage); and he later appears in revised form as a supporting character in *Splendor in the Grass.* Joker Evans, the delivery boy from the supermarket in *The Boy in the Basement,* appears as the same general type of character in *Glory in the Flower,* although the details of his presentation in the latter play are quite different from those in the earlier one; Viola in *Memory of Summer* bears broad resemblances to Lila in *A Loss of Roses;* and Bus Riley is suggestive in *Bus Riley's Back in Town* of Hal in *Picnic;* but, in *Glory in the Flower,* he more nearly suggests Bud Stamper in *Splendor in the Grass.* Inge's garrulous women who are used to fill in details (Lola in *Come Back, Little Sheba* and Lottie in *The Dark at the Top of the Stairs,* for example) are present in the persons of Mrs. Scranton in *The Boy in the Basement* and Mrs. Crosby in *The Tiny Closet.*

One-act plays serve Inge as exercises in characterization more than anything else. He claims that a number of his one-act plays "are fragments or sketches that I have written in exploration of

---

*References to *Glory in the Flower* (hereinafter referred to as *Glory*) are to the version of the play which appears in *24 Favorite One-Act Plays* edited by Bennett Cerf and Van H. Cartmell and published in 1958 by Doubleday and Company, Inc.

characters in larger works that I may or may not develop in the future" (x).* Of these one-act plays, only *Farther Off From Heaven, Glory in the Flower, The Mall,* and *The Strains of Triumph* have thus far received significant production, the latter three have been presented in the spring of 1957 by an amateur theatrical group at the University of Kansas.[1] There has been talk of an off-Broadway production of three or four of the one-act plays, but to date such a production has not come to fruition. Perhaps the 1962 publication of eleven of the one-act plays will stimulate sufficient interest to warrant more extensive production of some of them.

I To Bobolink, For Her Spirit

Bobolink Bowen, fat and fiftyish, her hair kinky, her eyes reduced to the size of buttonholes by the strong corrective lenses which she must wear, is an unlikely protagonist for a play. However, in Inge's portrayal of her, he demonstrates the kind of warm sympathy and understanding that he has for the undramatic members of his society. Created to be played by Shirley Booth at about the time he was writing *Come Back, Little Sheba,* Bobolink Bowen bears many physical characteristics common to Lola. Inge in no way sentimentalizes Bobolink, even though she is a rather tragic figure. He presents her with detachment, and he absolutely refuses to intrude upon the scene as author to make editorial comments. Bobolink appears to lead a useless existence, to which she has not only adjusted but in which she finds a modicum of excitement and satisfaction. She is the most venerable and successful autograph collector to haunt the sidewalk outside the 21 Club in New York. Within the narrow context in which she is presented, Bobolink has gained respect; indeed, she is looked upon as the final authority and arbiter in matters connected with filmland's famous citizens.

Perhaps Inge understood the Bobolink type and chose to write of it because he had always had a childlike awe of Holly-

*References to all of the one-act plays except *Glory in the Flower,* aforementioned, will be to *Summer Brave and Eleven Short Plays* published in 1962 by Random House.

wood stars. His own collecting of motion picture stars' pictures
was akin to Bobolink's collection of their autographs. In other
plays Inge shows his awe of members of the entertainment
world—Sonny, in *The Dark at the Top of the Stairs*, collects
pictures of film stars, and is especially interested when Sammy
reveals that his mother is in movies; Kenny in *A Loss of Roses*
says of Lila, "Gee, I never knew an actress before"; and Elma in
Bus Stop finds great romance in the discovery that Cherie has
worked in a night club.

From what Inge tells us in the play Bobolink does not live a
meaningful existence. The play has no real beginning or ending,
but is rather all middle. It is a slice-of-life presentation, and we
know nothing of the people assembled outside the 21 Club
except that they are all autograph hunters and that most of
them defer to Bobolink, the grand huntress, who is president of
the Irvington, New Jersey, Tyrone Power Fan Club. When
Renaldo begins to doubt that she actually saw Perry Como go
into 21, Bobolink, secure in her position, does not demean herself by arguing with him. Rather she haughtily tells him, "I said
Perry Como was inside, didn't I? If you don't believe me, you
don't have to." And Nellie, a great admirer of Bobolink, shows
more temper than Bobolink would ever lower herself to display when she says: "Bobolink knows a lot more about these
things than you kids do. She spotted Perry Como two blocks
away and Bobolink don't make mistakes. . . . You might remember that Bobolink is president of the Tyrone Power Fan
Club" (127).

If a reader of the play regards Bobolink as a sad figure, he is
doing so only because he tries to impose upon her his own
standards of what is worth-while in life. There is no indication
that Bobolink is dissatisfied with her lot. It is obvious that she
is psychologically immature, but she has created meaning in a
life which would probably be one of utter futility were it not
for her avid pursuit of famous names written on small sheets
of colored paper.

To Bobolink, For Her Spirit might well have been a cruel
commentary on the emptiness of lives such as the protagonist
and the other characters in the play lead. However, Inge does
not present the play in this light. He merely records something

which he has, in all probability, witnessed himself. He gives to the protagonist a pride and, within the framework of her circumscribed life, a dignity. This is especially notable when two well-dressed, beautiful people leave the night club and Annamarie, not knowing who they are, asks them to sign her book because she thinks they might be in pictures. But Bobolink is the professional: "this is small-time stuff for Bobolink. She has the dignity of her past career to think of. She stays back, leaning against the grill fence surrounding the club, with a look of superior calm on her face" (126). She then tells Nellie, "They might be famous *one* day . . . I said they *might* be . . . But I don't have time to waste on people that *might* be famous." That Bobolink should say this is ludicrous, but Inge does not use the line to make her seem ludicrous. Instead, he shows her acting within the boundaries of a propriety which she has established in order to give her existence at least some minor point. One can believe that someone like Bobolink exists; Inge presents her convincingly, and her motivations are well amplified within the limits of this short play. The completeness of her isolation is ever apparent.

The raw materials with which Inge was working in *To Bobolink, For Her Spirit* would lend themselves very well to satire; however, Inge is not comfortable in satirizing the common man— he respects ordinary people too much to take pleasure in dealing with them satirically. The closest that he comes to taking a satirical approach to his material occurs when Nellie, with Bobolink's prompting, tells the other autograph seekers about the time that Bobolink crashed the gate at Pennsylvania Station and got on the train which was bringing Tyrone Power from Hollywood. Nellie relates Bobolink's conversation with the actor on the train and then says, "He came hurrying through the gate with his coat collar turned up so no one would recognize him. I called out, 'Hi, Tyrone! I'm a friend of Bobolink,' but he started running." Bobolink somewhat takes the sting out of this remark, however, by volunteering, "He didn't want people to know who he was. Sometimes they get mobbed by fans and get their clothes ripped off and even get hurt" (125).

Within this play, Inge concentrates on depicting Bobolink, and the other characters are strictly supporting. However, a perceptive vignette occurs in the author's depiction of the doorman at the 21 Club. He is presumably of essentially the social class from which Bobolink and her followers come. But he is "a man of rigid and calculated dignity. . . . He holds head high and keeps it turned away from the autograph seekers as though to disclaim any association with them" (118). The doorman never speaks, but his failure to answer Fritz's question (119) tells the audience more about him than a great deal of dialogue might.

From a practical standpoint, *To Bobolink, For Her Spirit* is not a likely candidate for production. It is so fragmented as to be barely a play and is more accurately a group characterization. Its interest is largely historical; one who would explore the steps in Inge's development could not ignore the play because it gives a splendid insight into his method of character development, and the major plays are essentially studies in character. If the play has any theme, it is that of accepting one's lot as gracefully as possible. Bobolink does this. She receives ego reinforcement from Nellie and from the other characters who regard her as superior in her own small realm. If Bobolink has agonizing moments of loneliness and uncertainty, if she is disturbed by the futility of her life, Inge does not demonstrate this. He merely flicks the shutter of his camera and captures a moment in all time. Herein is the strength of his realism. The play is timeless and spaceless—it presents life suspended in a void.

II A Social Event

A Social Event is Inge's only published play which can legitimately be called a social satire. In it, the author writes of two rising Hollywood actors—they are man and wife—who must do the "right" things, be seen in the "right" places, and who have almost ceased to be people because everything they do is so contrived and so calculated. The play is short; but in the space of a few pages, Inge writes with enough witty cynicism to give it considerable impact. Inge is not nearly so bitter in this satire as Clifford Odets was, for example, in *The Big Knife;* but Inge exposes the falseness which he then thought typified Hollywood with perhaps a bit more success than Odets achieved in his Hollywood satire. Inge seems incapable of writing bitter and biting satire, primarily because he does not often use his art as an outlet for his aggressions. Occasionally these aggressions are apparent in an interview or in an essay which he writes; but he is too objective in his approach to his art to let them intrude in it. Also, as Tennessee Williams noted in the Introduction to *The Dark at the Top of the Stairs*, William Inge "uses his good manners for their proper dramatic purpose, which is to clothe a reality which is far from surface."[2] Above all else, Inge is instinctively a gentleman; and this quality usually shines through in his plays.

As *A Social Event* opens, Randy Brooks and his wife, Carole Mason, are just awakening in their ostentatious bedroom. It is ten-thirty in the morning, and Randy picks up the house phone to order breakfast from Muriel, the cook. Both Randy and Carole are upset because they have not been invited to a social event which is to take place at noon and "everyone in the business will be there" (152). The event, it soon develops, is the funeral of a well-known actor, Scotty Woodrow. The omission of Randy and Carole's names from the guest list is especially crucial to them because Randy has often been referred to by columnists as "the young Scotty Woodrow." And Carole's embarrassment is intensified by the fact that she has accepted an invitation from another actress to come by afterwards for a post-funeral gathering to "talk about what a great guy Scotty was, and everything" (154). But the most crushing blow of all is that "the guest list is going to be published in every paper in the country" (154). Randy and Carole, who represent complete egocentricity, feel that they can never live down the omission of their names from this list.

It is apparent that Randy and Carole expect reciprocity in matters which affect their careers. Randy, in a delightfully witty line, says, "I never knew him [Scotty] but everyone knows how much I've always admired him. In an interview just last week, I said 'Scotty Woodrow is still the greatest.' Now, I didn't *have* to say that . . . If you ask me, it showed a lot of humility on my part to say a thing like that when, after all, I've got a career of my own to consider" (153). On the basis of his magnanimous remark about Scotty, Randy thinks that he should receive some limelight by being invited to the funeral.

Randy plays every angle in trying to obtain the invitation, but time is running out. Finally, in desperation, he telephones again to his agent, who can do nothing for him. Then Carole, seeing no other way out, makes the irreverent suggestion that they could crash the party. But Randy, who vetoes this idea, feels that the only way out is to "give ourselves food poisoning. Just a light case. A little rotten meat would do it. Then we'd call the doctor and . . ." (155). But Carole rejects this suggestion; and, as Muriel arrives with the breakfast, it is obvious that the dreaded impasse has been reached. Randy and Carole are on the brink of admitting defeat and of not attending the funeral.

However, Muriel brings about the resolution of the play by reminding Carole that she will be off for part of the day. When Randy asks her, "Is this your day off, Muriel?" she replies, "No, Mr. Randy. I'm going to Mr. Woodrow's funeral" (156). She then explains that her mother worked for Scotty for years and that she was born in his beach house. She has been invited not only to the funeral but to join the family in the home after the funeral as well. Randy seizes the opportunity immediately and asks, "Muriel, do you have a ride to the funeral?" and, when Muriel says that she hasn't, Carole asks, "Look, Muriel, why don't we all go together?" (157). The play closes with Randy and Carole in a mad scramble to get dressed for the event. They are especially elated because Carole has to ask Sandra to be excused from her post-funeral gathering in order that she and Randy may go back to the Woodrow home with "a few of his very closest friends" (159). Randy quite typically ponders whether it will look all right to go to the funeral with the cook, but he concludes, "I guess it'll look all right. After all, funerals are very democratic affairs" (159).

Despite its brevity—the play is just eight pages long—*A Social Event* makes several points. Chief among these is the crassness with which some people work toward gaining success in the acting profession; to them, no action is any longer spontaneous. A funeral becomes, as Carole states, not "a social *affair* exactly, but it's a social *event*" (155). The only real allusion made to the deceased is one by Randy who, in a line which might have come from a Nichols and May sketch, says, "He was really great. It makes me very humble to think of a guy like Scotty" (154). But

Randy's humility is as ephemeral as a hot day in London. And besides, he never knew Scotty.

Carole's remark about what Sandra is going to wear to the funeral is also tellingly satirical: "Sandra had an entire new outfit made. Perfectly stunning. And she had the dress made so that she can have the sleeves taken out later and wear it to cocktails and supper parties. After all, black is a very smart color now" (153). The only shreds of sincerity in the play are found in the actions of the principals in pushing their own advantages. Even Muriel does not seem overly distressed at Scotty's death. No one really expresses any emotion even barely resembling grief, even though Carole says the conventional thing to Sandra: "Oh, it's all going to be terribly sad" (159).

One final point which Inge makes in the play is that everyone appears to be living a lie and that those who lie are very suspicious of everyone else, thinking that no one is truthful—which may be true. When Randy asks how Anne and Mark came to be invited to the funeral, Carole reminds him that Mark once played Scotty's son in a film; and Randy, after thinking for a moment, speculates. "That means Mark's a little older than he admits" (154). Also, when Carole says that everyone will be at the funeral, Randy reassures her by saying, "It could be some of the others are lying about their invitations, too. You realize that, don't you?" (155).

The material which Inge uses in this play is nicely adapted to a brief presentation. The play does not have sufficient material or variety to be anything more fully developed than a one-act production. Despite its brevity, *A Social Event* is conventional in dramatic structure and has a more clear-cut form than has *To Bobolink, For Her Spirit*. *A Social Event* has a definite beginning in which the basic problem is stated with admirable verbal economy, a well-sustained middle in which the problem is grappled with, and a clearly defined ending in which the problem is neatly resolved. The anti-climax, which occurs in the last eight speeches, is used to highlight the hypocrisy of the principals in two distinct ways: first, Randy ponders whether it will look all right for the cook to go to the funeral with them— an ironic but expected twist—and, secondly, Carole's rather haughty telephone call to Sandra asking to be excused from the invitation which she has accepted.

A Social Event is Inge's most atypical play in setting, characterization, and basic philosophical and dramatic approach. His realism is underplayed in this work, and his sense of whimsy—which keeps the play from being bitterly satirical—is more highly developed than it has been in any of his other published work.

III   The Boy in the Basement

The most convoluted of Inge's one-act plays is *The Boy in the Basement*, which is a sympathetically told story of Spencer Scranton, a mother-dominated, middle-aged, homosexual mortician. Spencer lives with his mother and his father, a paralytic who is stone deaf—perhaps hysterically deaf because he cannot stand to hear his wife's constant chatter—and who makes no utterance in the two scenes of the play other than "Uh," but who provides a contrast to Joker Evans as well as clues to Mrs. Scranton's personality. Spencer is a dutiful son, and his duty has deprived him of the chance of making any sort of life for himself. He tries not to appear resentful, but it is obvious that he knows he is missing a great deal in life. He tells his mother, "they all get to lookin' pretty much alike. One dead body after another. That's all life gets to be" (165).

Spencer's only diversion is his weekends in Pittsburgh, the nearest large city. Mrs. Scranton has apprehensions about these weekends, but she prefers to close her eyes to anything which might confirm her deepest fears and suspicions. However, as the play opens, she reveals some of her suspicions which have been brought to the fore by the fact that last weekend Spencer had to telephone her in the middle of the night and have her immediately wire him two hundred dollars on the pretext that his car had needed repairs. She has been mulling this incident over uneasily and has reasoned that any reputable garage would have waited until morning for the money. She then asks Spencer point blank, "Were you with a woman?" When Spencer answers that he was not, she says, "No, you never took to women the way your brother did. Well, maybe he taught you a lesson. You see where he's ended up, don't you? A mental hospital for the rest of his life. And what sent him there? Whiskey and women. Whiskey and women" (166). In this speech is revealed the essence of Spencer's situation—he is caught in a trap. He tries to protect his family from the sort of injury which his brother brought upon them and asks only that he be allowed a little life of his own. He asks only a modicum of privacy, much as Mr. Newbold does in *The Tiny Closet*.

Mrs. Scranton, a pillar of society, is self-righteous and upright. She feels her civic responsibility very strongly and is a key member of the local ladies' club. As she goes off to the weekly meeting of this group, Spencer tells her to have a good time; but she responds, "We ladies don't have these meetings to have a good time. We must accomplish things. To try to keep some semblance of order in this godless little mining town" (167). She then goes on to say that the ladies are now on a crusade to drum out of town any movies which do not meet their circumscribed moral standards. When Mrs. Scranton leaves, Joker Evans, the delivery boy from the supermarket appears on the scene to deliver an order of food. Joker, who also appears as a delivery boy in *Glory in the Flower*, is a thoroughly likable boy of eighteen. He is now finishing high school and is going to college on a scholarship he has just received. He hopes one day to become a doctor. Joker is thoroughly and genuinely fond of Spencer who kids with him and has a deep affection for him. Joker bounds in and says, "Man, it's great to be alive, a day like this" (169). He engages in pleasant banter with Spencer and at one point tells him, "I can have as much fun talkin' with you as with any guy my own age" (173). Joker represents the young, hopeful type who is faced with the possibility of spending the rest of his life in the constricted confines of a small mining town if he doesn't leave and obtain an education. He tells Spencer, "I just gotta get to college if I ever wanta get outa this town" (171). The hope that Joker expresses here is what was denied Spencer in his youth; he had to come back to the mining town and to his parents, because of his sense of duty.

Spencer is ever aware of his father's difficult situation. Mr. Scranton is being punished by his wife, now that she can take advantage of him because of his utter dependence upon her and Spencer. In Mrs. Scranton's eyes he apparently has not been the model husband. Among other things, he has drunk; but now not even beer is kept around and he has little opportunity to drink. Spencer, however, keeps liquor in a bottle labeled embalming fluid; and, when Mrs. Scranton is out, he gives his father a drink. Just as he does this, the sound of the car is heard in the driveway, and Spencer quickly puts away the bottle saying, "Her Royal Highness. She's back" (175).

Mrs. Scranton enters looking as though she had been given "a glimpse into some far truth she had never before quite realized." She tells of how she had to leave the meeting at which she was presiding when she learned that the Hi-Ho Bar—Spencer has a package of matches from the bar—was raided on the very night that Spencer telephoned and needed two hundred dollars at once. She tells Spencer, "you called me for two hundred dollars to pay the policeman to keep him from putting you in jail and to keep your name out of the newspaper. . . . And the police raided the place because it's a meeting place for degenerates . . . [a place] where men meet other men and join together in . . . in some form of . . . lewd depravity" (176-77). Mrs. Scranton's tirade is enough to bring all of Spencer's long accumulated aggressions to the fore; he takes a suitcase and stalks out of the house, vowing never to return again. Thus ends the first scene as the tension builds to a climax.

The second scene takes place early the next morning. Hoping that Spencer will come home, Mrs. Scranton has sat up all night. As dawn breaks, his car comes into the driveway. "He is defeated and knows it. And his bearing tells us he accepts the fact, although sadly" (179). The Oedipus conflict between mother and son comes to the fore with Spencer's return. The directions indicate that "All the fears and resentments they have fought inside themselves during the past several hours are purged now in a fast embrace. Their need, their desperate dependence on each other, their deep love bring them together like lovers" (180). Mrs. Scranton immediately re-establishes her hold upon Spencer by telling him that, had he not returned, she would be ready for the basement (the embalming room). Then she exacts from him a promise that he will never leave her again and says, "it's like we'd made a pact together, a long time ago. If one of us breaks it, we're both destroyed" (180). Even at this moment when Spencer has returned, Mrs. Scranton, more by instinct than by design, asserts her control upon the situation and takes unfair advantage of her son.

A significant clue to Mrs. Scranton's motivation is given when, in her longest tirade in the play, she declares: "I've loved my son since the day he was born and kept him to my breast with loving care. I think I even loved him more than I loved my own husband, for my son's infant love was innocent and pure, and demanded no fleshly act to satisfy its needs" (177). Mrs. Scranton, who says that she has "fought so hard for the right! . . . fought so hard to keep my mind and heart and body *pure* and free from all physical craving" (177), *has* fought too hard. She actually hates men, and the strained marriage relationship which she had with her husband has caused enough tension in the home, one might surmise, for Spencer to have no desire for marriage which, subconsciously at least, has come to be represented by the only marriage of which he had any extensive knowledge, that of his mismated parents. Spencer, then, comes to represent the dutiful, respectable man who lives constantly with the guilt of his homosexuality and with the frustration of his unfulfilled longings.

The Boy in the Basement cannot be said to have a subplot, for the Joker Evans part of the play is just as integral to it as is the Spencer-Mrs. Scranton conflict. The question of Spencer's homosexuality precipitates the climax of the first portion of the play. And the audience's knowledge of this problem makes especially pathetic and poignant the second climax: the death of Joker Evans. It is apparent that Spencer loves Joker but that he is far too honorable to introduce Joker to the homosexual experience.

The death of Joker Evans is symbolic. When Spencer returns home after his debacle with his mother, he soon learns from Mrs. Scranton that a corpse is to be brought in for preparation. Spencer complains, "One dead body after another. That's all my life is." Then he asks his mother, "How did you know I'd be back?" and she smugly answers, "I . . . I thought . . . you would be" (181). The body is brought in, and Spencer discovers that it is Joker, who has been drowned. He can only repeat the boy's name incredulously. He goes into the morgue and "finally moves from his frozen stance at Joker's side to rub one soft hand over the boy's chest, as though it were precious metal" (184). When Mrs. Scranton calls down suspiciously to ask him what he is doing, he replies bleakly, "You'd be suspicious if I was in the same room with a stuffed owl" (184). The curtain falls with Spencer saying, "Jesus Christ, Joker, I wanted you to live" (185); then he severs Joker's main arteries, "feeling the pain of doing it to himself" (185).

Spencer's last line is most significant. In saying that he wanted Joker to live, he implies that Joker represents all that is worth living for. Joker is the same sort of symbol that Little Sheba is, but Joker represents hope and freedom rather than innocence; he realized the necessity to break away. But his hope was killed aborning. When Spencer returns home, he is done for. His mother, a thoroughly destructive woman, will consume him; after she is dead, her overpowering influence will reach from the grave to haunt Spencer. He will now never overcome her.

Inge is highly successful in showing the contrast between real sensitivity and adherence to conventional standards of behavior. Early in the play, Spencer has been preparing the body of an old woman who has burned to death. Mrs. Scranton wants to hear the details of the woman's death; when she is told that "one whole side of her [was] raw and purple," she makes a face and says, "Poor old lady. Did you fix her up to look all right?" (164). Spencer tells his mother that "she looks like a chorus girl now," and Mrs. Scranton is shocked. She upbraids her son for speaking disrespectfully of the dead. But when Joker is brought in, Mrs. Scranton, who makes a point of stressing to her son that this is to be a cheap funeral, goes on talking about how she is fixing eggs for breakfast and "contented as a new bride, sings 'Rock of Ages'" (184). She then calls Spencer and, in a line which depicts human insensitivity better than any line in modern American theater, shows precisely the unfeeling, brutal sort of woman she is: "You can eat your breakfast while he's draining, can't you?" (184).

Mrs. Scranton is probably the most satisfactory character that Inge has ever presented. She is a complicated woman, and Inge uses every possible nuance to sharpen the audience's image of her. The complications of the play proceed convincingly from the situations which Mrs. Scranton has created. *The Boy in the Basement* has excellent psychological insights; besides this quality, it is a warm and moving drama, made intense by the abbreviated form in which it now exists. If Inge does not turn this play into a full-length drama, the loss to American drama will be great. The one-act play which now exists is a promising nucleus from which to build toward a major drama on the same basic theme.

IV   The Tiny Closet

Many of the basic psychological conflicts present in *The Boy in the Basement* are also present in *The Tiny Closet*. While overt homosexuality is not the major issue or the precipitating factor in this play, it is apparent that Mr. Newbold is a homosexual and presumably a very much repressed one whose life is largely one of withdrawal.

Mr. Newbold, a floorwalker in a department store in a Midwestern city, lives in a boardinghouse run by Mrs. Crosby, a compulsive talker and a supreme hypocrite. He has rented his room with the understanding that he may install his own lock on the tiny closet in his room and that no one will ever go into it or try to discover its contents. Mr. Newbold apparently does not know enough about human nature and about landladies to realize that his understanding with Mrs. Crosby would be quite enough to make her break the door down if necessary to see what was being hidden in this closet in her highly respectable Victorian house.

When Mr. Newbold first appears on the scene, he has great difficulty in stopping Mrs. Crosby's word flow long enough to castigate her because he has found evidence that someone has tampered with his lock. Mrs. Crosby is so ready with protestations of her own innocence and with possible explanations of how the lock came to be tampered with that there is no doubt in anyone's mind that she is the culprit.

Mr. Newbold's life is very neatly summed up in one speech which he makes to Mrs. Crosby: "a closet is a very small space. That's all I ask in this life. That's all I ask, just that tiny closet to call my own, my very own" (190). The audience is told nothing of Mr. Newbold's past; it sees very little of his present; and it has few grounds for speculating on his future. The center of the play is that this well-groomed, obsessively neat man wishes the small amount of privacy which the tiny closet affords.

Mrs. Crosby is quick to assure Mr. Newbold that he will have no further difficulty about keeping his closet private; and, before he leaves to go to work, she tells him "you're my favorite of all the roomers. Oh, I wish they was all like you. You keep your room spotless, and you're always so correct around the house. My, you're my model guest" (191). But, as soon as Mr. Newbold has left, Mrs. Crosby gets on the telephone and tells her friend Mrs. Hergesheimer to come right over so that they can proceed to rifle the lock on which they have already been working for some days. Mrs. Crosby speculates on what might be in the closet. She can't believe that Mr. Newbold is a Communist, but then one never can tell. And she hardly thinks that he is storing love letters there because he doesn't seem the type.

Mrs. Crosby returns to the supposition that he might be a Communist, but she says to Mrs. Hergesheimer, "He belongs to the Lions' Club. Do you think he'd be a Communist and still belong to the Lions' Club?" Mrs. Hergesheimer, ever vigilant, replies, "You can't tell. Lots of them join clubs like that just as a cover-up. That school teacher I got—she's a Red and I know it. Brings home all kinds of books to read. Yes. Dangerous books. But she goes to church every Sunday morning, just as big as you please, just to pretend she's *not* a Red" (195).

The result of the conversation is that the two women convince themselves and each other that they have not only a right but a duty to invade Mr. Newbold's privacy and go into his closet. Just as they are doing so, Mr. Newbold, who has suspected that this sort of thing would happen, returns. The directions indicate that "he is very nervous. His heart is pounding. He starts up the stairs and then comes down again. He can't seem to get the courage to confront the women" (196). Meanwhile, the women get into the closet and find there not a pile of love letters, not an arsenal, but "Hats! Dozens of hats!" (197). Mrs. Hergesheimer, quite unwilling to believe that Mr. Newbold has come by these hats honestly, proclaims: "He must have brought them home from the store, don't you think?" But then they notice that there is also sewing equipment in the closet, and it is evident that Mr. Newbold spends his spare hours making hats. The two women now come downstairs, carrying some of the hats with them. Mr. Newbold ducks into a closet to hide. He is able to hear all that Mrs. Crosby says: "He . . . he's just peculiar. That's all. He's just peculiar. . . . He's too prim for a man. He's too tidy the way he keeps his room. It's just not natural. . . . Why, I'd rather be haboring a Communist. . . . I'm going to ask him to leave" (197-98). She goes on to say that she is going to call the department store in which he works and tell his employers what sort of man they are employing.

The ending of the play is artful. The expected clash between Mr. Newbold and Mrs. Crosby does not come. Were it to come, it could hardly be much more than a repetition of the audience's first encounter with the two, except that Mrs. Crosby would now be more openly vengeful. Rather, Inge has Mrs. Crosby try on an elegant hat and make all sorts of gestures before the mirror "with a feeling of low burlesque" (199). She then exits, as has Mrs. Hergesheimer; and Mr. Newbold comes out of the closet. "He is a shattered man. All of his pride, his erect posture, his air of authority are gone. He has become a shy and frightened young girl. Lovingly, he picks up the hat and carries it to the mirror where he puts it on, looking at himself" (199-200).

The Tiny Closet is ultimately concerned with human dignity and with the sanctity of one's privacy. Mrs. Crosby takes the role of surrogate mother, and her self-righteousness emphasizes her similarity to Mrs. Scranton in *The Boy in the Basement*. Mr. Newbold is living with a problem to which he has adjusted relatively well, as has Spencer Scranton. But Mr. Newbold has a distinctly rigid personality; Spencer Scranton, on the other hand, had a more flexible personality; he showed no indications of acquisitiveness, but indeed indicated a great generosity of spirit. Essentially Inge has investigated two classic types of homosexual personality in these two plays, and in the second has complicated the basic condition by superimposing upon it the additional element of fetishism with a base of transvestism. Despite the psychological complexities of *The Tiny Closet*, the personality of Mr. Newbold is totally consistent psychologically and is highly convincing. The entire play is presented in a minor key, and the greatest dramatic impact probably occurs for most people *after* the final curtain at which Mr. Newbold—whose name is most ironic—"falls onto the sofa and cries like a hopeless child" (200).

Inge has a continuing concern with man's right to privacy, and he also introduces into a number of his plays the question of censorship. He does not develop the latter theme very extensively and often uses it primarily as a means of character delineation. However, it is evident that the anti-Communist activities of the McCarthy era were important motivations to Inge and that much of the social impact of his plays can be best understood in the light of McCarthyism. The most direct and sustained example of his attitudes about individual liberty and freedom of choice is found in *The Tiny Closet*, a play which in the space of eleven pages systematically strips naked the soul of a sensitive man who is in quiet conflict with the mores of a hostile, self-righteous, suspicious, and destructive society.

Perhaps there is not sufficient dramatic material in *The Tiny Closet* for a full-length production; Inge states in his preface to the edition of his one-act plays that he regards the play as complete. However, one would certainly hope that he will work the characters of Mrs. Crosby and Mr. Newbold into some future work, for each is presented with unusual verisimilitude and clarity. *The Tiny Closet* succeeds admirably because it is an unusually quiet presentation of a highly explosive situation. In no other play does Inge succeed any better in presenting the desperation and clutching loneliness of modern man. The closet becomes the symbol of man's only security—the return-to-the-womb implication—but this security is violated by those who, in the name of duty, destroy it.

V Memory of Summer

Memory of Summer (of youth) has about it an atmosphere suggestive of *Come Back, Little Sheba* and of *A Loss of Roses*. Viola, the play's central character, is much like Lila in *A Loss of Roses;* but Viola hasn't Lila's grip on reality. Viola is described as "a slim woman in her forties, with a delicate prettiness" (203). She is apparently the wife of a well-to-do man from St. Louis. During the action of the play, she is at a seaside resort with

Alice, her old housekeeper, who now is more nurse-governess to her than housekeeper.

As the play opens, Alice is trying to persuade Viola not to go for a swim. The air is cold, and swimming is dangerous since it is past Labor Day and the beach is no longer guarded. But to argue with Viola is quite impossible because she is obviously out of touch with reality and cannot be appealed to reasonably. Alice would be most relieved if her charge would consent to acknowledge that summer is over, but Viola can only respond, "Nonsense, Alice" (204). Alice reminds her that "You have a husband and a fine home waiting for you in Saint Louis, Miss Viola. Why don't you come back to the cottage with me now, and we'll make our reservations and start our packing." But Viola will not consent; "It's my holiday," she tells Alice.

Viola cannot accept the fact that her youth is over. She is attempting to prolong summer, to turn her back on the blatant fact that fall is approaching. She attempts to identify herself with youth, but she succeeds only in making herself look foolish. Viola's personal isolation is quite obvious from much that she says. She tells Alice that she likes to have her breakfast and then "hurry to the beach, where all the young people are laughing and playing and . . ."; but Alice reminds her, "Miss Viola . . . there aren't any young people here now. There's no one here now" (204).

Viola has romantic dreams that tonight she will "be dining at the inn, and the inn will be full of young people, beautiful young people, dancing . . . I want to look *young* for them, Alice. And I'll dance with the young men, too. And I'll laugh for them. And I'll tell my naughty little stories for them, my naughty-nice stories, to amuse them" (205). Alice hopelessly reminds her that "there's no one at the inn. The orchestra played its last dance on Labor Day." But Viola doesn't permit herself to hear this. Then she turns and runs into the surf.

At this point a young Coast Guardsman blows his whistle and shouts to Viola that she must come out of the water. Alice runs off to call the doctor, and the Coast Guardsman is left with a beach blanket in which to wrap Viola and a flask of brandy with which Viola can warm herself. When Viola comes from the water, the Coast Guardsman tells her that she cannot swim there any more. Viola's response is a typical Blanche DuBois response: "I must say, I appreciate your thoughtfulness and concern. It's most gallant of you, but . . ." (208). But the young man punctures this romantic balloon by telling Viola, "It's not gallant, Lady. It's just my orders."

Memory of Summer does not really end; more accurately, it plays out. Viola tries to win the affection of the young Coast Guardsman but is rebuffed. She goes back to the cottage to await the arrival of the doctor Alice has called. At the final curtain, she is still talking about looking her best for the young people tonight. The conflict of the play is without resolution. This is not a dramatic weakness; it is merely the author's indication that some situations in life, as unsatisfactory as they are, persist.

The conflict in the play is largely an ideological one. Romance —or fantasy—is pitted against reality. The Viola image is set in a broader and more universal framework than the Blanche DuBois image. Blanche represents the fading of the Southern aristocracy, and her retreat into unreality comes about because of this. But Viola represents the more universal problem of the loss of youth. She is emotionally immature, as are many of Inge's women—Lola, Cherie, Lila, Claire Brinkman. However, Viola is the most extreme example of emotional immaturity in any Inge play. If his other female characters have shown their emotional immaturity by retreating from reality, they have been drawn up sharply before the play ended and have been forced to come to grips with reality. But Viola is not responsible for her actions; she has built her own psychological fortress and dwells therein. She is an example of almost total egocentricity; her solipsism forbids the existence for her of anything outside her own imaginings.

Inge's presentation in this play is highly objective. The reader of the play is not made to feel sorry for Viola, who is happy within her self-created world. She is not aware of her condition and is content with her dream world. She is well looked after and enjoys the warm and gentle protection of Alice. One might rue the elements which have led Viola to her present state; but Inge does not deal with causes except in the most oblique way— for example, he notes that Alice has been with Viola since Viola's early childhood, indicating that possibly Viola has always needed looking after. On the other hand, Viola is married; and one can hardly think that any man would have married her had she been this pathologically unrealistic from earliest childhood. It is more likely that Alice was just an old family servant who became Viola's servant when she married. Inge presents effects; but, if one feels pity for Viola, he can do so only by feeling empathy for her.

In one sense, Inge's title is ironic. Viola will always be young. One is what he thinks he is, and Viola is stalwart in identifying herself with youth. Were Viola not pathological in her refusal to face reality, the play might be very sad and pessimistic. But as it stands, the play is neither pessimistic nor optimistic. Rather, the situation just *is;* and Inge, the objective recorder, presents it as it exists.

Memory of Summer is not a very notable play; it is more an autumnal tale than a play. As a drama it has hardly any forward thrust, and the entire action boils down to talk. The play, nonetheless, is a thoughtful piece and an interesting experiment.

VI Bus Riley's Back in Town

The Hotel Boomerang was built to serve a boom town in the middle of Texas. However, the town's prosperity has boomeranged; and, when the play opens, the hotel bar is all but deserted. Howie, the barkeep, talks with a salesman who remembers that it "used t'be I'd come into this town and sell maybe five thousand dollars' worth a merchandise in one day. . . . I'm doing good now if I make my expenses" (215). Howie and the salesman provide the background for the main plot of the play, the reunion of Jackie Loomis and Bus Riley who were lovers when they were seventeen and eighteen years old, respectively, and who have not seen each other for five years. Jackie would have borne Bus's child had not her father interfered and insisted upon an abortion. He then had Bus jailed for corrupting the morals of a minor, for Jackie was a child in the eyes of the law and Bus was a man. Bus has not been back in town since this series of events; however, he has now returned because his father has been desperately ill and needs blood transfusions which Bus can give him. Meanwhile, Jackie's father, who once was the town's richest man, has lost nearly everything, is in declining health, and has been drinking excessively for years. Jackie, still unmarried, looks after him; and she still longs for Bus whom she deeply loved at the time she became pregnant.

Bus has been in town for several days but has made no effort to reach Jackie. She now comes to the bar of the Boomerang to find out from Howie all she can about Bus. She is determined to see him even though her friends Bernice and Ralph—who have no legitimate dramatic function in the play other than to provide background—wish to prevent a meeting between the two. Jackie gets her friends to take her home just after Bus enters the bar. He does not notice Jackie; but, as soon as she gets home, she drives back in her own car to have her long-awaited meeting with him.

Now a member of the United States Navy, Bus is handsome in his uniform. This is his last night at home, and he is eager to get away from the dull little town which he left in such bitterness five years earlier. He has now seen something of the world; Jackie, in contrast, has led a dull and reclusive existence looking after her father. Bus is pent up from the strain of being at home and of his father's illness. He wants to find "action" tonight, and he talks with Howie and the salesman about the possibility. All the girls he used to know are either married, living elsewhere, or dead. But he scrupulously avoids asking about Jackie, and it is Howie who finally brings up her name and tells Bus that she has been asking about him. At about this moment, Jackie's car pulls up outside; and Bus starts to leave—"I'm heading out the back way. I can't see Jackie again" (229). Howie urges Bus to stay, and this delays him just long enough that he cannot leave without seeing Jackie.

It is soon clear to the audience that there have never been any hard feelings between Jackie and Bus, but that Bus, having once run head-on into trouble with Jackie's father, wants to take no more chances. However, he and Jackie soon decide to go to the next county to buy a bottle, and Bus suggests that they might stop at Riverview, a roadhouse on the way. Before they leave, Bus and Jackie dance together, and Jackie tries to talk about the past but does not find Bus responsive. The past has been so bitter that Bus wants only to forget it; Inge makes very clear that its bitterness has made Bus feel incapable of loving anyone. Bus tells Jackie at one point, "I don't fall in love any more" (233), and later in the play that "Love, to me, is something they put you in jail for" (239).

Bus soon makes clear to Jackie that he wants to take her to the Riverview and spend the night. He makes no pretense of still being in love with her, and she is taken aback by his proposition. She tells him: "Bus, you used to love me. I know you did. But you can't even pretend to now. You've just been making up polite answers to everything I've said. I'm just any other girl to you now that you can . . . can let off steam with, and then forget it" (236). Jackie still wants to recapture the past—"Oh, Bus, can't you remember the way we used to feel?"; but, failing in her attempt to do so, she leaves the bar. However, she reconsiders and decides that, if she can't recapture the whole past, she can at least recapture some of it; and she returns to go off to Riverview with Bus. This is not exactly the redemption-through-sex ending of such a play as *The Dark at the Top of the Stairs,* for there is little suggestion of redemption; but it is a more honest and credible ending than one finds in most of Inge's major dramas. Jackie takes what happiness she can find, and she makes any necessary compromise in order at least to get something.

Bus Riley's Back in Town does not report directly a crucial moment of desperation in the life of man; yet it is a play of sustained despair in a minor key. The crux of desperation has been reached and is now far in the background. The characters in the play no longer have enough passion in them to experience emotional intensity. The boom town has died, and with it the youth and hope of the characters have faded. Bus will not allow himself to relive the emotion which led to his imprisonment. Five years earlier he had loved Jackie—just as Bud Stamper had loved Deanie Loomis in *Splendor in the Grass*— but the beauty and essential purity of this love are negated when society (Del Loomis and the courts) moves against it. When Bus says that he will finish his drink so that Howie, the barkeep, can close up, Howie answers, "No hurry, Bus. Take your time. I gotta stay open until midnight, anyway, whether there's customers or not" (238). In this statement is mirrored some of the desperation of the characters in the play. One has to live out his life, and life becomes lonelier as one passes through it.

Inge has often had difficulty in presenting necessary background material in a natural and convincing way. In *Bus Riley's Back in Town,* he is considerably more deft than usual in providing background. The introduction of Ralph and Bernice (219-25) was not entirely necessary to the dramatic development of the play; however, the salesman reminisces very convincingly with Howie early in the play and reveals to the audience a great deal of necessary detail about the past. Then Jackie, who hasn't seen Bus in five years, fills him—and the audience—in on more details; and the providing of background material becomes a structurally integral part of the play. *A Loss of Roses* and *Bus Stop* would have been stronger had a comparable expository technique been used in them.

One minor theme that serves no apparent purpose is introduced in *Bus Riley's Back in Town,* and the author would have done well either to develop it or drop it entirely. The audience is told that Bus's mother is a Mexican (223), and Bus speaks later in the play of going down to the Mexican district to pick up a girl. Since the author's purpose in introducing this additional touch is ill-defined and totally unrealized, the play would be tightened by omitting it. One is given no reason to believe that Del Loomis' resentment of Bus is based upon the fact that he is part Mexican. Howie has already given the audience the clue to Del's resentment: "Del was crazy about [Jackie]. He acted to me like he was jealous of the boy and in love with her himself" (219). Having introduced this complication into the play, Inge might have pursued it rather than suggesting obliquely other conflicts and complications.

It seems ironic that Bus, who is back in town to give his father blood transfusions, should be very eager to leave. He tells Howie, "I'm clearin' outa here in the morning. . . . I've had enough of this town, forever" (225). What the town most needs —young people like Bus to pump new blood into it and to give it new vitality—it cannot attract; and this situation sets the tone for the entire play. Del Loomis has crumbled, both as a force in the town's business and as a person; but he has made sure that he will not be replaced and that with his decline and death the town will decline and die. In Del's decline, both physical and economic, there is a definite feeling of just retribution; however, Del has had the last say in the town which he had built.

Many of the imperfections of *Bus Riley's Back in Town* have been corrected in *Glory in the Flower* which is essentially the same story. This rewritten version of the play, however, is dramatically tighter than the original play as will be shown in the following discussion. The Ralph-Bernice sequence is omitted in the rewritten version, and this omission adds to the directness of the dramatic impact. The introduction of new characters and significant changes in the presentation of the principals also give the later version increased focus and credibility.

VII Glory in the Flower

In *Glory in the Flower* are found numerous suggestions of characters and incidents from a number of Inge's other plays. The "flower" referred to in the title is represented by roses which Jackie wears in her hair in an attempt to look younger than she is. At the end of the play "She throws her roses on the floor, disgustedly" (150), and this action marks her coming to maturity. She has found maturity now only because she has finally come to the full realization that she is no longer in love with Bus Riley. She must face life on realistic terms after twenty-odd years of living a romantic fantasy about Bus. The throwing away of her roses is directly equivalent to Lola's giving up her search for Little Sheba and is suggestive of the significance which roses played in *A Loss of Roses*.

Jackie strongly suggests many characteristics which Inge attributes to Lila in *A Loss of Roses*. Jackie is about Lila's age: "She is a woman nearing forty, but pretty, with a clear, fair skin and a pleasing fullness about the body, and a sweet, girlish smile that makes her attractive. Jackie has tried to keep her youthful looks and succeeded. At this particular time, perhaps she has tried too hard" (135). Inge also suggests that Jackie has an attachment to Joker, an eighteen-year-old boy in the play, which could develop into something passionate; but there is no suggestion that the relationship has yet reached that stage. By the end of the play, Jackie has gained enough perspective that she is able to tell Joker, "Right now, I feel very old, and I'm kinda proud" (149).

Joker is brought over by Inge from *The Boy in the Basement;* however, in this play his close association is with Jackie rather than with an older man. Joker is a strong motivating character in *The Boy in the Basement,* but his primary function in *Glory in the Flower* is that of providing contrast. He and his young set provide a mirror to Jackie and Bus's past; and, by using his minor characters in this way, Inge is able to omit considerable dialogue about the past.

Glory in the Flower, like *Bus Riley's Back in Town,* strongly suggests portions of *Splendor in the Grass;* and in *Glory in the Flower* Inge even goes so far as to have Jackie recite the portion from the tenth stanza of William Wordsworth's *Ode on Intimations of Immortality* which contains the words "splendor in the grass." The first version of the Bus Riley–Jackie Loomis romance is closer to *Splendor in the Grass* than is the same romance in *Glory in the Flower* because the original version presents Del Loomis as the vengeful parent who interfered with the two young people. In *Glory in the Flower,* nothing is said about Bus's having been imprisoned because of Jackie's pregnancy; instead, the audience is left to think that he just left town when he realized that a complication had developed in his romance.

In rewriting and recasting his original material, Inge gave his play a directness which had been lacking in the first version. To begin with, he does not have Jackie appear to be on the prowl for Bus. Bus has telephoned her, and they have agreed to meet at the Paradise Bar. Jackie appears on stage first and does not attempt to fill the audience in on the past in any detail. Rather, she acts in such a way that the audience can size her up as she now is. She talks with the young people—Inge says in his directions, "She sounds like a kid herself" (136)—and dances with Joker. The salesman and Howie are at the bar, just as they were in *Bus Riley's Back in Town;* but they do not provide the audience with much background. The only hint of background which they provide before Bus appears on the scene is a tantalizing bit when Howie answers the salesman's question about whether Bus is her husband by saying, "No . . . Bus wasn't ever her husband" (137). The answer obviously implies that there is more to be said, but Howie is not about to say it and is effectively prevented from being questioned further by Jackie's return from the dance floor. All that the audience gleans about the past comes from the two principals in the play, Jackie and Bus. The author deals much more frugally with his background material than he has in many of his other plays, and the dramatic effect is heightened by this restraint in presenting details.

Inge gains a great deal by making Bus and Jackie about forty years old rather than twenty-three or twenty-four as he originally had. This age makes the past more remote and allows Bus to be presented as a less bitter character than he was in *Bus Riley's Back in Town*. When Bus and Jackie come together in the present play, each has found his own life much more decisively than either had in the early version; Jackie leads a rather dull existence as a piano teacher, but she has adjusted to this. She has had various boy friends and has had the opportunity to marry. Bus, who has been living in California, is a small-time boxer and a bit actor. He gives an exciting account of his life in California; and, while this account is very hard to believe, it is obvious that Bus has grown far beyond the little town in which he was born. The two principals no longer love each other, but each has sentiment for their mutual past. And in *Glory in the Flower*, Jackie declines Bus's request that they spend the night together. She leaves, then returns to the Paradise, just as she had returned to the Hotel Boomerang; but in this play, she merely returns to make sure that there are no hard feelings on Bus's part. They shake hands, and Jackie leaves. This ending, on the whole, is more satisfying dramatically than was the more typically Inge ending of *Bus Riley's Back in Town*.

Glory in the Flower emphasizes the theme of perpetual change. The salesman's opening line is: "Nothing ever stays the same" (135). Later in the play he tells Howie, "There oughta be a law to keep things the way they are" (142). The salesman's reminiscences in this play are most often used to promote the theme of the play, but in *Bus Riley's Back in Town* they are used to promote the plot by providing background detail. Both plays are concerned with the inroads which time makes, but the longer term view which is possible in *Glory in the Flower* gives greater force to Inge's ideas. The later play also ends on a more optimistic—and realistic—note; Jackie has made a step toward maturity—and it is a convincing one inasmuch as her romantic image has been shattered. In both plays, change has meant decline; however, in the ending of *Glory in the Flower,* there is a reversal of this attitude. The resolution does not come about in the pat, happy one typical of much American drama; instead, it is a facing of reality and a gaining of dignity by Jackie: she feels old, and she is proud.

Glory in the Flower is most interesting for the way in which it presents Jackie. In *Bus Riley's Back in Town,* she lacked pride. She went out to find Bus and she yielded to him in the end telling him, "I'll be . . . just an ordinary girl . . . you happen to pick up . . . and we'll throw a ball" (239). But Inge establishes Jackie's pride early in *Glory in the Flower*: Bus has telephoned her, she maintains her pride throughout the action. In both plays Jackie's characterization is consistent, but in the later play it is more completely convincing.

VIII   The Rainy Afternoon

The Rainy Afternoon, a fragmentary study of childhood, is tenable psychologically. Two little girls, ten-year-old Wilma and seven-year-old Billie Mae, are spending a rainy afternoon playing in an old barn in a small Midwestern town. They are dressed up in their mothers' dresses and high heels. It is soon apparent that Wilma, the older child, is an aggressive little brute. She and Billie Mae each have dolls, and she tells Billie Mae, "You've got to spank your baby to make her behave" (243). Billie Mae protests that her doll is behaving, but Wilma forces her to spank the doll and scold it.

It is apparent that Wilma hasn't many friends and that she is possessive of those who are in her clutches. When Billie Mae wants to leave because she is having no fun at their make-believe tea party, Wilma accuses her of not knowing how to play. However, when ten-year-old Vic Bates enters the scene, Wilma immediately relegates Billie Mae to the background.

Billy Mae tries to be a part of the conversation between Wilma and Vic, but she doesn't stand a chance. Wilma argues with Vic over whether his father's car is better than her father's car, and she then suggests that they play house. Wilma is to be the mother, Vic the father, and Billie Mae alternately the baby and the maid. Billie Mae protests that her mother doesn't want her to play with boys, but Wilma assures her that what her mother doesn't know won't hurt her.

The action proceeds as the children play house—Hubby comes home from the office, and he and mother chatter on. Wilma, true to form, says that baby (Billie Mae) has been very bad today and must be spanked, whereupon Vic spanks her with Wilma on the sidelines urging him to ". . . spank her hard, Hubby dear. She's been a very bad girl" (247). Billie Mae very understandably objects to her role in the game, so Wilma sends her to bed. After a few speeches, she recasts her as maid.

The game—and the play—moves along rather tediously until Wilma becomes the pubescent enchantress who suggests, "You've had such a busy day at the office. I think you should go to bed now and be sure to get your rest. . . . Our bedroom is in the hayloft. We'll go up there and leave Baby down here" (251). Vic, totally uninterested in this proposition—boys mature later than girls—would rather go out for a walk, but Wilma blocks his escape by reminding him that "You can't. It's raining outside" (251). She then taunts him with the accusation that he is scared, and this leaves him with nothing to do—if he is to save his manhood—but follow the eager Wilma to the loft.

Meanwhile, Billie Mae is feeling "lonely and rejected" (253). She can get no response from the two in the loft, so she leaves crying, vowing that she will never play with Wilma again and threatening to tell her mother. Her final utterances are "I hate you, Wilma Wadsworth. I'll never be your playmate anymore. I hate you. I hate you" (254). The stage is left empty, and Inge suggests that "There are several minutes of absolute and mysterious silence" (254).

One cannot take *The Rainy Afternoon* very seriously. It is merely an exercise in characterization and only as such does it succeed. The plot is trivial and there is no well-developed theme in the play. It is a study of part of the growing-up process, and Inge has had considerable interest in this process throughout his work. Whereas a number of his major protagonists come to maturity in middle life in the plays in which Inge is concerned with emotional maturity, here he is concerned with physical maturity, and Wilma is in the midst of achieving this during the action of the play.

The Rainy Afternoon is rather like an Inge parody on Inge. When Wilma virtually drags Vic into the hayloft, one thinks of the ending of *The Dark at the Top of the Stairs* and wonders whether Inge did not write this short play with the longer one in mind. One wishes that Inge might capitalize upon his understanding of children by introducing more of them into his major work. To date the only young child in any of his plays is Sonny Flood, and he emerges as a less convincing child than do the children in *The Rainy Afternoon*.

IX   The Mall

The Mall, another of Inge's slice-of-life plays, takes place over a very short period of time, probably not more than twenty minutes. Set at a seaside resort after the close of the season, Inge uses the setting to suggest the autumnal atmosphere of the play. His directions indicate that "the time is early fall . . . and the park is out of season." Summer is past and there is a feeling of rejection in the atmosphere: "behind the promenade are the banners heralding the freaks" (257). These banners look mockingly upon the scene, as do the two live freaks, the two old crones who are on stage during the entire action of the play and who serve to give unity to what transpires.

In *The Mall* Inge attempted "to write a play that made its dramatic point by a kind of combustion of forces rather than by a real narration. I had just wanted to contrast certain kinds of love and dramatize people in their pursuit of love" (256). In the short space of this play, Inge examines six specific types of love. The old crones, a pervasive element in the play, represent lost love. They still long for love and lecherously watch the scene before them in order to experience vicariously some of the love which it presents. One crone tells the other that "any type's *my* type, Sister" (261); and she also says, "It's *always* time for the lovers, Sister. Love goes around the clock" (260).

The two matrons exercising on the beach represent conventional married love which has cooled with the years but is socially acceptable. They are shocked by the old crones and by the lovers in the play. They and their marriages are characterized by what one of them says about the approach of autumn: "in September, you know the summer's over and wintertime is ahead, and the weather will be cold" (258). These two women are probably less fulfilled in their existences than the two old crones who at least have some lurid memories to live on. By introducing the two matrons very early in the play, Inge sets up his contrast between them and the crones; and he emphasizes this contrast in a speech which one of the crones makes, mocking one of the matrons: "'I have to go home now and fix something for the children. Junior needs all his strength 'cause he's layin' the new maid, and little Geraldine is always hungry when she gets back from the opium den'" (260).

The most hopeful presentation of love in the play is that between the sailor and the young girl. These two have a healthy attachment for each other; but, as in *Bus Riley's Back in Town* and *Splendor in the Grass,* parental objections stand in the way of love. The girl, just seventeen, tells her nineteen-year-old swain, "I been out late the last three nights, and the folks are beginning to suspect something" (265). The two, who have found a sort of identity in each other, want only to be together; but to be so is not possible for them. Inge infers here, as he often does in other plays, that the best possible love, young love, meets so many obstacles in the course of its fulfillment that the innocence and excitement which are a part of it are killed by the difficulties which it encounters.

In the characters of Barney, Dell, Clara, and the middle-aged man, Inge presents three faces of love. Barney has recently been released from a mental hospital, where he presumably landed because he was not able to cope with the rejection which he received from a middle-aged streetwalker named Clara. Now, out of the hospital but still in a precarious mental state, he returns to the mall where he knows Clara will be soliciting. He wishes to live with her and to recapture the love which he had once experienced: "I know what real love *is*, Clara. I had it once, long time 'fore I met you. It was wonderful, Clara. My life was hers and her life was mine and we had real happiness together" (269). But Clara is not the type to settle down, especially with Barney for whom she has a great antipathy. Clara, who represents the sort of person who equates love with physical experience and who wants as much variety as possible, is on the mall awaiting the arrival of a man with whom she has a date for the night and whom she will probably never see again. She counters loneliness with casual affairs. But Barney cannot accept her promiscuity, and he grabs her passionately, much as Bo grabs Cherie in *Bus Stop*, telling her, "God damn it, you're goin' with me. I got real love in my heart and I'm gonna learn ya what it is. You'll be happy after you know" (270-71). But Clara, understandably annoyed and perhaps frightened as well, "kicks Barney in the groin and slaps at him viciously" (271).

Barney is accompanied to the mall by his erstwhile friend and companion, Dell, who is much like Virgil in *Bus Stop*. Dell represents the love of a close friend, the outgoing love which is selfless and which is motivated by the genuine concern and interest of one human being for another. Dell is, therefore, paternal and protective. When Clara attacks Barney, Dell tells him to fight back, even if she is a woman; but Barney tells him, "I can't fight . . . A man in *love*, Dell, has got no fight" (271).

The Mall is actually a modern morality play, and the crones are almost medieval figures. They are used well to reflect all of the emotional states which the action brings about: they weep at young love; are mocking when conventional, middle-class love is presented in the persons of the two matrons; and are gluttonously curious about the many loves of Clara. The crones, "as weathered as the benches and the scenery surrounding them" (257), are a pessimistic presentation of what aging involves. They are made lecherous by their unfulfilled desires. Ugly as gargoyles, they are a grim reminder of what life holds. Inge makes his intention clear by having Clara say, upon entering the scene, "Why don't you old hags go off somewhere and die? Why don't you old witches get on your brooms and ride off into the sky? Old hags! Too old to have any fun yourselves. All you can do is sit here makin' fun of others" (268). Her speech, as it continues, shows Clara's own fears and insecurities: "*I'll* never be like you. I'm still young. And I still got what it takes to make 'em take a second look. And I'm gonna have my fun."

The pervading atmosphere in this play is one of loss and loneliness. Every character is trying to hold back time or to recapture the past, and in essence every character is alone. Even the sailor and his girl, who love each other in a way which would provide fulfillment for them, must face the objections of her family and the fact that they will be separated for a year. No one in the play really has any sort of fulfillment to look forward to except Clara who goes off for the night with her middle-aged Lothario; but her solution is short term and the audience is made fully aware of what sort of life she faces in the long term.

Inge's microcosm is well chosen, for it emphasizes the passing of youth in much the way that deserted beach in *Memory of Summer* does. The faded posters of freaks and the empty buildings support Inge's theme throughout the play. Life is constantly passing; and, with each minute, man becomes increasingly alone. Between some people, love just happens (the sailor and his girl); others seek love frantically as Barney does. But there is an impediment to all love, and no love is permanent. The conclusions which one is forced to reach after reading this play make Inge's first four Broadway productions seem hopeful by comparison; for in each of them there is at least some suggestion that the principals will not go through life enduring the total isolation which appears to be the inevitable lot of the characters in *The Mall.*

X An Incident at The Standish Arms

An Incident at The Standish Arms tells of the mid-afternoon seduction of a hapless taxicab driver by a respectable society divorcée and is chiefly concerned with the guilt which the woman feels when the affair is over. Inge does not give names to the characters in this five-and-one-half-page, one-act play. It is doubtful, indeed, that the man and woman involved know each others' names. The play essentially involves only two characters, although the woman's twelve-year-old daughter appears and has two brief speeches at the conclusion of the play.

The woman represents a totally different social milieu than the man. She is well-to-do and appears to have considerable social status. The man is presented in sharp contrast to her socially. But ironically, it is the man who has an inherent pride and dignity; the woman—perhaps through her affair with the taxi driver but more likely on account of deep-seated feelings of guilt—has lost her self-respect. She apparently builds up to the point at which she must have physical satisfaction with a man; but, once the immediate satisfaction is attained, she is so overcome by guilt that she cannot bear to face the man. She also lives in fear that her young daughter might come home while the man is there or that the management of The Standish Arms might become suspicious because a taxi driver came from her apartment.

As the play opens, the woman enters the stage from the bedroom. Inge indicates in the directions that "she can only clutch at the air blindly and stifle the compulsory screams in her throat. There being no magic exit, she finally runs to a corner of the room like a guilty child seeking her own punishment" (277). Throughout the play the woman seems cornered and trapped, but not by the man—she is cornered by her own fear and guilt, she is "seeking her own punishment." Her animal desires are in constant conflict with her equally strong desire to be a good mother and a respectable woman.

The man is a sympathetic character. The woman has vamped him, and he has yielded to her vamping. However, he has made no advances, and he is in no direct way a threat to the woman. He makes his position clear to her when he says, "Look, lady, I got a family, too. I got three kids. Yah. I don't want trouble no worse'n you do" (278). When the man stays to have a drink, he recounts for the woman—and the audience—the particulars of their meeting. The woman in no way denies that she has led him on, but she seems somewhat shocked by his recounting her methods. Finally, the woman asks her lover to leave by way of the service elevator so that he won't be observed. He reluctantly assents to do so, but he asks for a kiss before he leaves. The woman says, "Not now. I . . . I couldn't" (281), and at this point the play reaches its dramatic climax; the man, angry and insulted, seethes at her, "Then God damn you and your hypocrite ways! To hell with you and all your kind. (He seizes a costly Chinese vase from a table and flings it to the floor.) You've made me feel cheap, God damn you! You've made me feel cheap" (281). The irony, of course, is that this man, upon whom the woman looks as a social inferior, shows his inherent dignity and, in this speech, reveals that he has a better opinion of himself than the woman has of herself. He is infuriated, too, because he spends his life in a position which is obviously inferior to that of most of the people whom he serves and in which his individual dignity is not recognized or appreciated.

The woman explains her indiscretion by saying, "I get very lonely at times, since I was divorced, and I . . . I miss my husband in these ways" (280). But her guilt overwhelms her completely after the man has smashed the vase and left. She falls to the divan sobbing, "Oh, God, what makes me do these things? Dear God, what makes me do them?" (281). Hearing her daughter at the door, the woman assumes "her normal respectable posture" (281). When the daughter enters, she ironically asks her mother to write a note to her teacher asking that her seat be changed at school "because there's a perfectly horrid girl who sits across from me. She uses all sorts of filthy words, and she stinks because she never bathes, and she wears ugly, dirty dresses" (282). The woman promises to write the note for her daughter, thus bringing the presentation of upper middle-class hypocrisy full circle. The daughter's speech also explains some of the mother's great guilt and fear in regard to her affair.

Short though it is, *An Incident at The Standish Arms*, which has never been produced, is a sharply focused social vignette in which the commentary is biting and rather bitter.

XI   The Strains of Triumph

Inge's title, *The Strains of Triumph*, is taken from the last verse of Emily Dickinson's "Success Is Counted Sweetest." The second word in the title has the double meaning both of "sounds" and "burdens." The play revolves around a love triangle involving two athletes, Ben and Tom, and the girl both of them love, Ann. The triangle is vaguely reminiscent of the Turk-Bruce-Marie triangle in *Come Back, Little Sheba* and of the Hal-Alan-Madge triangle in *Picnic*. Tom and Ann wish to be friends with Ben even though romantically he is now left quite out of the picture.

Inge introduces Professor Benoit, an associate in Classics, into the play to provide a generalized parallel to Ben. Professor Benoit tells Ben—note the similarity of names—that he was once in love, but "it terrified me. She was so beautiful, so tender, so fine that I trembled in her mere proximity" (291). In the same speech, the longest in the play, Professor Benoit states his theory that "all people are divided into two groups, those who participate and those who watch and observe. Sometimes . . . I wonder if I have lived life at all, if my life has not been, rather, a period of observation on earth, watching others live." Ben, who has always been in the races which he and Professor Benoit are now seeing from the hillside, feels "humiliated just to stand and watch" (298); but Professor Benoit, returning to the sentiments he has expressed earlier, tells Ben, "Oh, come now. One doesn't have to run in the races to enjoy them. Sometimes I think I enjoy the relays more than anyone, standing up here on my lonely hillside" (298).

One would certainly have to grant that what Professor Benoit says gives but the meagerest comfort to the distraught Ben. Few people would care to be a Professor Benoit, standing on a lonely hillside all alone except for casual passersby, watching the vitality which unfolds before him. But Ben, quite unconvincingly, finally comes to agree with the professor that "From here, it's beautiful and exciting" (299).

The Strains of Triumph is lacking primarily in intensity. Ben's agony does not succeed in being convincing, and one always has the feeling that Ann, as she is presented here, is just not worth the effort of even the feeble agonizing which is seen. The story begins with an unfortunately diffuse focus. Professor Benoit is seen, but at first he is merely a figure. Ann and Tom occupy the center of the audience's attention, and the play, presumably, is to be theirs. They discuss how they have fallen in love and how Ann must jilt Ben in order to be pinned to Tom. The professor, who rankles at having been referred to by the two as "just an old man," hears what has gone on and sees the love play which Ann and Tom engage in before they leave the stage.

When Ann and Tom have left, Ben appears on stage like a wounded steer. He has either overheard Tom and Ann or has gleaned what the situation is. The voluble professor meets Ben's agony head-on by talking compulsively and by awkwardly and unconvincingly relating to Ben the essentials of his past history. Ben is in tears, and the professor rants on frenetically, baring his soul. In the background are the sounds of the meet which is taking place on the athletic field. Prominent in the sounds is a variety of victory yells, and the most meaningful of these, repeated several times throughout the play, is "Give 'em the axe, the axe, the axe!" which is, of course, what Tom and Ann have done to Ben.

In this play Inge again deals with the spontaneously aroused love which has afflicted such earlier characters as Madge and Marie. He again shows that someone must be hurt by this love, but for the first time he tells his tale from the viewpoint of the injured rather than from some other viewpoint. However, Professor Benoit serves as an intermediary between the lovers and the rejected lover, much as Lola did in *Come Back, Little Sheba*. The blithe magnanimity with which Ann and Tom would reach out their hands in friendship to Ben shows their utter lack of sensitivity to his feelings. Tom goes so far as to suggest almost cruelly to Ben that he come to the varsity dance with them tonight: "If you don't have a date, you can dance with Ann all you want to . . ." (295).

Inge attempts to make a parallel between the competition of athletics, in which both of the younger male characters are involved, and that of love. Professor Benoit supports this parallel when he speaks of the race in such terms as to indicate both the athletic event and the race which Ben and Tom have been running to win Ann. However, the parallel is never successfully drawn, largely because it is overdrawn and because there is little freshness in it.

Were the play to be expanded, the character of the professor would have to be recast somewhat; for Professor Benoit—like Professor Lyman in *Bus Stop*—is seriously defective. In fact,

Inge's approach to professors is generally stereotyped. When, in *Glory in the Flower*, professors from the state university warn the town that the mines will give out because the mineral veins are shallow, the town disparages this judgment because, as Howie clearly indicates, "Who listens to professors?" Charles Barrett is probably correct in his judgment that "the fact that he [Inge] sacrificed his acting career which he wanted so badly in order to prepare himself to teach is probably of significance in his later attitude toward the teaching profession in his plays."[3]

The Strains of Triumph, like most of Inge's plays, deals with banal people and with a banal situation. Usually Inge can vivify the banality of the situation by means of his depth of perception; however, these depths seem not be be plumbed in this play.

XII *The Shorter Plays*

In writing of Inge's first published one-act play, *To Bobolink, for Her Spirit*,[4] Charles Barrett quite correctly states that "The play closes *status quo*. . . . There is not an iota of difference in the characters when they are finished with their brief moment on the stage than there was from the characters when they entered. They assume identical positions to the ones they had in the beginning of the story."[5] What Barrett says regarding one play, might be said of all of these one-act plays. The only difference between the first play and most of the others is that, before the return to virtually the same identity, most of the characters in the later plays pass through some crucial situation. It must be granted that the characters in *The Rainy Afternoon* undergo some sort of change, but this play represents the coming to awareness of two children and the disillusionment of a third—which is perhaps another part of awareness. Even in *The Tiny Closet*, which closes really just as the crucial situation is met, the presumption must be that Mr. Newbold will go back to his solitary life of desperation, although he will probably do so in a different rooming house and possibly even in a new town.

The pervasive problems with which Inge is concerned in the one-act plays—as well as in the full-length productions—are loneliness and personal isolation. The existence of his characters "is vicarious, and their minds have slipped out of step with the times to a mild degree. They are escapists from reality. They are certainly not people with whom an average audience can find empathy. They are people who are smaller than the currently popular 'little people' of drama."[6] The character who best personifies the vicariousness of which Barrett speaks is Lola; however, the crones in *The Mall,* Viola in *Memory of Summer,* Mrs. Crosby and Mrs. Hergesheimer in *The Tiny Closet,* Bobolink Bowen in *To Bobolink, for Her Spirit,* and Spencer Scranton in *The Boy in the Basement* are all living vicariously as is Elma Duckworth in *People in the Wind* and in *Bus Stop.*

Inge demonstrates an ability to write satire, although, as has been mentioned, he has for the most part avoided doing so. *The Social Event* is his only thoroughgoing satire, and it is refreshingly satirical because it is not bitter nor especially cynical. *The Incident at The Standish Arms* is partially satirical, but the play becomes more nearly a character study than a satire. Inge is obliquely satirical in his passing allusions to women's clubs in *The Boy in the Basement,* and in *The Mall* he satirizes the clubwoman type in the two matrons. He returns to this type of satire in *The Rainy Afternoon* when the children are playing house and Wilma, role-playing the society matron, says, "I guess you weren't invited to the big party at the country club yesterday. All the society people were there. I wore a beautiful new dress to it. Mrs. Sylvester Jones was there. She's a cow. She was dressed in horrible clothes. And her manners are terrible" (244). This statement has shades of statements made about Mary Jane Ralston in *The Dark at the Top of the Stairs* and in *Farther Off From Heaven.* In general, Inge almost subconsciously satirizes the country club or the women's club set which apparently represents to him a very false element in modern society. He does not editorialize about these groups; but it is altogether possible that he may some day write a play about them as satirical and witty as *The Social Event.*

Adrienne Reeves has pointed out that in Inge's four major successes the author has emphasized physical appearance, and that the physical appearance of the characters is often the key to understanding the frustration of the major character—Lola's untidiness, for example.[7] Physical characteristics become very important in the presentation of the characters in the one-act plays; and, as has been noted in the case of Mr. Newbold in *The Tiny Closet*, they become definite psychological clues. Inge's keenest observation of physical characteristics—and their attendant implications—is found in the one-act plays.

In most cases, to read a one-act play by Inge is to glimpse a sketch or an unfinished painting by an artist—to catch, as it were, the artist in the process of creation. The plays discussed in this chapter indicate Inge's method—his careful observation, his faithful recording, his detachment, his writing from character rather than theme. Most of Inge's plays are highly indicative of his ultimate concern with the forgotten people of society: the most commonplace of the common, the least likely to be heralded or remembered, the loneliest of the lonely, the quietest of the quiet, the least noticed of the suffering.

CHAPTER 5

Lampsacan Shrines?

WILLIAM INGE, in 1953, was referred to as "Broadway's white hope."[1] While this was the opinion of just one small town reviewer of his work, his being awarded the Pulitzer Prize and other significant honors in that year led most critics to admit that Inge was a potent force in the American drama of the mid-twentieth century. Even his severest critics could not fail to note some of his strengths. Theophilus Lewis called Inge's receipt of the Pulitzer Prize an honor which exceeded "all recent efforts to achieve absurdity."[2] However, he could not deny that Inge "has a sharp eye for observing the processes of life" and that he understands the "carpentry" of his art.

Inge has constantly been referred to as a member of the dramatic triumvirate which includes Tennessee Williams and Arthur Miller, and his name is decidedly established in American theater. After his first play had been produced, a number of New York critics regarded him as America's most promising recent playwright; and many thought that the vigorous, vital theater of the 1920's and 1930's was now to return under his leadership.[3] To an extent their sanguine expectations were fulfilled in *Picnic*, in *Bus Stop*, and in *The Dark at the Top of the Stairs*, even though with considerably less dynamism than most of them had originally envisioned. But nearly a decade later, many of these same critics pounced upon Inge for the dramatic failure of *A Loss of Roses*; feeling that their expectations had not been met in the plays which followed *Come Back, Little Sheba*, the critics still could not deny the great popular appeal of the three plays which followed it. However, in noting the patent weaknesses of *A Loss of Roses*, many of the critics gave vent to what seemed to be years of bitterness, and some attacked Inge with a genuine personal vengeance.

It is apparent in all of his full-length plays up to and including *The Dark at the Top of the Stairs* that Inge was concerned with producing commercial successes. Success has meant a great deal to Inge who, as late as 1962, said, "I can never understand this idea that a writer shouldn't try to make money."[4] However, the artist who specifically sets out to make money, must often do so at the expense of his art; and Inge has made some artistic concessions in order to make his plays commercially successful. His changing of much of *Picnic* at Josh Logan's urging is an indication of the sort of concession that he was willing to make.

Paul Green has said that "The American theatre is not dying. It is still alive and flourishing as it never has been. Only the Broadway theatre is dying. . . . The people's theatre is no longer an extension of Broadway. Rather the reverse. Broadway is a part of the people's theatre and only a part."[5] Green, in turning his back on Broadway and Hollywood, has continued to produce in accordance with his own dramatic standards. However, Inge has not yet been able to wean himself away from the success goddess; he aims to please, and the last few years have been trying for him because he has not enjoyed the sort of critical response which his early years in drama brought him. As early as 1957, Charles Barrett wrote that "Inge's promise is in his writing plays for theatre and drama—not Broadway."[6] In *Natural Affection* and in a number of his one-act plays, Inge has written with his own artistic integrity more in mind than popular appeal. *Natural Affection* was made sensational in the hope of enticing audiences; but the bulk of this sensationalism could be dropped from the play and what remains would be better drama than one finds in Inge's first four Broadway productions. Were Inge to expand *The Boy in the Basement,* retaining the restraint and understanding that are evident in the one-act version of the play, it is altogether possible that his artistic integrity would come into close harmony with audience appeal.

I Inge's Themes

The most well-developed themes in Inge's plays are those of loneliness and personal isolation. These problems are, of course, the thematic substance of an overwhelming number of modern plays. However, in only a handful—*Death of a Salesman, Cat on a Hot Tin Roof, A Streetcar Named Desire, Member of the Wedding, Who's Afraid of Virginia Woolf,* and *Tea and Sympathy*—is the theme so dominant and so consistently developed as it is in the plays of William Inge. It is virtually impossible to find a single Inge play—full-length or one-act—in which the characters are able to communicate with each other in any but the most rudimentary way. And genuine attempts to communicate are usually awkward beyond description—as in the case of Bo's attempt to communicate with Cherie in *Bus Stop,* or Professor Benoit's attempt to communicate with Ben in *The Strains of Triumph.*

From the themes of loneliness and personal isolation grows the theme which indicates that man must compromise if life is to have any hope for him. None of the plays ends on a note of real optimism, for even in *Summer Brave* and in *Bus Stop* the heroines follow their men to very uncertain futures; and one comes away from these plays not with the feeling that Inge has solved any problems but that he has chosen to end the play right at the beginning of a major problem. This tendency is one of the many sides of Inge's Realism; however, this Realism is quite unconvincing in the ending of *The Dark at the Top of the Stairs*—Rubin and Cora will have their night together, but this cannot change the sixteen or seventeen years during which they have lived together; they will have to face a tomorrow that will be just as bleak as today. The ending of *Natural Affection* abandons any attempt at Realism in any dramatically valid sense and ends sensationally.

The redemption-through-sex theme which pervaded the earlier plays is absent from *Splendor in the Grass* and from *Natural Affection.* Indeed, in the latter play, sex becomes a most destructive force; it stands in the way of Sue's performing her obvious maternal duty of taking Donnie into her home. The redemption-through-sex theme is also absent from a goodly number of the one-act plays. Even in those one-act plays which are overtly concerned with sex—*Bus Riley's Back in Town, The Rainy Afternoon, The Mall,* and *An Incident at The Standish Arms*—there is no suggestion that sex offers any form of redemption.

Inge has been severely criticized for the emphasis upon sex in his plays. Eric Bentley asks, "Why can't he see through the popular fallacies of priapism and give himself to his own impulse for genuine domestic comedy?"[7] However, a large part of Inge's thematic development is dependent upon the very priapism which Bentley objects to. The loneliness and isolation of Inge's characters lead them to reach out for whatever human contact they can achieve, and this contact is more often achieved through sex than through real understanding.

II *Inge's Gallery*

Inge's themes and plots are all developed essentially from his character sketches which are largely the product of his keen, highly objective observations. Inge has said that he feels a duty "to find all that I can in the human lives that I know and are available to me—and find the meanings in those lives secondarily. I'll always have to work that way rather than to take a theme and work in the characters secondarily."[8] The one-act plays give ample evidence that what Inge has stated is completely true, for the one-act plays are largely character sketches with no contrived theme. In them, theme is arrived at naturally and somewhat spontaneously as a product of the carefully developed characterization.

William Inge is usually the conscious Realist in his writing; however, when Romanticism overtakes him, as it occasionally does, he leans toward Naturalism. Whether he is being essentially a Realist or a Naturalist at any given time, he depends almost wholly upon sharp characterization for the presentation of his ideas. Such authors as T. S. Eliot, Clifford Odets, Elmer Rice, Edward Albee, and often Eugene O'Neill use their characters as vehicles for the presentation of their ideas, but William Inge concentrates on creating Rembrandt-like portraits from which ideas necessarily proceed. Tennessee Williams and Arthur Miller are similar to Inge in permitting theme to evolve essentially from intricate character delineation.

Inge is at his strongest in depicting female characters, and his ability in this area has been generally recognized.[9] Most of his female characters have dominated the men with whom they are associated and the resolution of most of the plays has come about when the men have finally been humbled by the women. Inge, who has never married, shows a fear of feminine domination; but in his plays he points to the inevitability of it. The battle of the sexes is predominant in his plays; and the woman is, with rare exception, the victor. Essentially Inge's women are bent on showing their independence—Rosemary, Sue Barker, Helen Baird; or they are bent on emasculating their men so that they can dominate them and thereby bolster their own egos: Lola, Lottie Lacey, Cora Flood, Sue Barker, Mrs. Loomis, Mrs. Scranton.

Inge's first major male character was much overshadowed by his wife. Lola was the undeniable center of *Come Back, Little Sheba;* and Doc, despite the large number of lines which he was given and the high drama of his drunk scene, could not compete with her. In his next play, Inge created in Hal a figure of considerably greater dramatic stature than Doc. Howard, in *Picnic,* was also a strong supporting character, although Alan was never fully realized. By the time Inge wrote *Bus Stop,* he again permitted his male characters to fade somewhat, and the spotlight was largely on Cherie. However, Virgil was a sensitively portrayed secondary character. Professor Lyman was something short of convincing—as was Professor Benoit in *The Strains of Glory.* Clark Kerr has recently written that "The faculty member is more a fully participating member of society [now], rather than a creature on the periphery; some are at the very center of national and world events."[10] Certainly Inge's professors do not fit such an image. They are largely spectators: people who have no fundamental contribution to make to society and who are unconvincing as human beings, always on the periphery.

The chief male character in *The Dark at the Top of the Stairs* is Sonny Flood. Rubin Flood and Morris Lacey are, by the very nature of the play, squashed by their mates. Inge permits Lottie to describe Rubin before his emasculation, but the audience sees him only in futile protest to Cora and in his eventual return and humiliation. As the curtain descends, the audience can have absolutely no doubt that the family's destiny is now in Cora's hands.

Kenny Baird is a Sonny Flood type of character in many ways.

He tries to dominate his mother who, like Cora, is inconsistent in dealing with these attempts. Sonny had tantrums; but Kenny, being several years older than Sonny, instead has an affair with Lila—his form of rebellion against his mother and also, Inge suggests, his means of salvation. Donnie Barker is generally of the same cloth as Sonny and Kenny, and his rebellion—the senseless murder of a woman—is the most violent.

Inge has gained great control over his characterization in the years that he has been writing, even though there are still some notable defects in it, as, for example, his placing too much importance upon the Helen-Kenny problem in *A Loss of Roses* to the neglect of Lila. He is in much better command of his characterization in *Natural Affection* in which one must admire especially the control with which the characters of the subplot, Claire and Vince Brinkman, are presented. They are convincing, yet they do not usurp the spotlight from Sue Barker and Bernie Slovenk.

Inge is most successful in portraying people of the lower middle classes, and he is most convincing when he is able to set them in the Midwestern atmosphere of the 1920's. His few excursions outside this class and this time have been somewhat strained, although such short plays as *A Social Event* and *An Incident at The Standish Arms* are both promising in their satirical approach.

III *A Matter of Viewpoint*

Inge's point of view is largely that of lower middle-class Midwesterners of the 1920's or the early 1930's. In most of his plays, his audience does not take sides, nor is it expected to. There are no "heavies" in Inge's plays; even the less sympathetic characters are presented in such a way that the audience can feel compassion for them—the loneliness and insecurity of Professor Lyman, the pride and inner turmoil of Ace Stamper, the apparent sincerity of Bernie's Slovenk's love for Sue Barker. Inge rationalizes the behavior of each character by using a somewhat composite viewpoint within each play.

The objectivity of Inge's presentations is almost scientific. The clinical approach is consistent throughout the plays but it is not coldly so. Inge permits the characters to make their own explanations, and he never directly leads one to make any moral judgments which he, as author, has preconceived.

IV What Immortal Hand or Eye?

The structure of William Inge's plays has been carefully calculated and has usually followed the Aristotelian principle that each play have a definite and clearly defined beginning, middle, and end. Generally speaking, the three dramatic unities are also observed scrupulously in all of Inge's work except in his scenario writing.

Inge has taken liberties with some basic dramatic principles, but he has done so with good reason. For example, in Come Back, Little Sheba, the beginning is extraordinarily protracted and the play temporarily becomes dull. However, this makes the climactic action of Doc's drunk scene the more effective. The middle of this play is somewhat telescoped, and the end is brief and direct. A great deal of the play's dramatic effect is dependent upon the distortion which is here apparent.

The plays are strong in fundamental progression which John Howard Lawson considers to include the decision, the grappling with difficulties, the test of strength, and the climax.[11] The test of strength, which Lawson calls the obligatory scene, is the center of every Inge play, both full length and one act. This scene contains the expected clash—for example, Sue Barker's finally facing the necessity that she had to choose between her son and her lover or Madge's yielding to Hal's advances. The obligatory scene is followed in the climax by the final clash which, in the examples above, would be Donnie's committing murder or Madge's losing Alan.

Inge is successful in establishing his context before introducing his crucial conflict. Because he is writing of people whose dramatic stature would normally be considered slight, he has to create a convincing context and to allow his audience the opportunity of identifying with it before the conflict can be convincingly crucial for them. Inge has, through tight structural control, turned commonplace materials into the sort of Americana which one finds in a Grant Wood painting.

V *Critics' Choice?*

Contemporary critical judgments about artists of all kinds have been notoriously shortsighted and patently incorrect throughout history. From Martial to Whitman, from Euripides to O'Neill, from Bach and Beethoven to Hindemith and Menotti, from Cimabue and Da Vinci to Picasso and Rivera, critics have made poorly supported and dimly illuminated judgments. Therefore, judgment by any mid-twentieth-century critic about William Inge should be looked upon as highly suspect—including that of the present volume; for historical perspective inevitably alters contemporary opinions. Also, in the case of William Inge, no final critical page can be written until all of the data are in; and hopefully the playwright will be producing for many years to come. This volume is on Inge's extant work but may actually be on only half or a quarter of what will one day be his total production.

At present, Inge has proved himself to be capable of writing thoughtful and provocative works which have considerable mass appeal—and this statement is a matter not of judgment but of historical fact. His phenomenal decade of success extending from 1950 to 1959 has been temporarily eclipsed by two successive Broadway failures.

Inge's ear is carefully attuned to the dialogue of the people he writes about. He does not have Williams' gift for poetic dialogue; however, he has demonstrated a unique ability to transmit through dialogue the crushing boredom and the ensuing frustration of singularly commonplace members of society. Inge's Kansas and Oklahoma become extensions of Lewis' Main Street; of Anderson's Winesburg, Ohio; or of Wolfe's Dixieland. In a sense Inge's Realism becomes a notable form of American Gothic. In Inge's work, the dark recesses are in the human mind rather than in the landscape and architecture; the eerie stone buildings become bungalows in the great American flatland; the horror is less bloodcurdling than sustained; the blacks and the whites of human behavior tend toward grays.

William Inge remains a gifted artist, a consummate gentleman, a warm and sensitive creator. He continues to feel a strong sense of responsibility to his audiences, and one devoutly hopes that his next production will bring him into a closer harmony with them than has been evident in the past five years.

Notes and References

Chapter One

1. "The Men-Taming Women of William Inge," *Harper's Magazine*, CCXVII (November, 1958), 52.
2. *Idem*.
3. Milton Bracker, New York *Times*, March 22, 1953, II, 1.
4. "Mr. Inge Looks Back," New York *Times Magazine*, November 24, 1957, p. 80.
5. Bracker, p. 3.
6. See *4 Plays by William Inge*, pp. v-vi.
7. "Talk of the Town," *New Yorker*, XXIX (April 4, 1953), 25-26.
8. Bracker, pp. 1, 3.
9. "New Play in Manhattan," *Time Magazine*, LXX (December 12, 1957), 42.
10. Tennessee Williams, Introduction, *The Dark at the Top of the Stairs*, pp. vii-ix.
11. Bracker, p. 3.
12. Williams, p. ix.
13. Bracker, p. 3.
14. *Idem*.
15. Phyllis Anderson, "Diary of a Production," *Theatre Arts*, XXXIV (November, 1950), 58.
16. *4 Plays by William Inge*, p. vi.
17. William Inge, "Concerning Labels," New York *Times*, July 23, 1950, II, 1.
18. William Inge, "*Picnic*: From 'Front Porch' to Broadway," *Theatre Arts*, XXXVIII (April, 1954), 33.
19. William Inge, " 'Picnic': Of Women," New York *Times*, February 15, 1953, II, 3.
20. *4 Plays by William Inge*, p. ix.
21. *Ibid*., p. x.
22. Volume LXV (March 14, 1955), 58.
23. See Inge's comments on this, *4 Plays by William Inge*, p. vii. See also Henry Hewes, "Mr. Inge's Meringueless Pie," *Saturday Review*, XXXVIII (March 19, 1955), 24.
24. Naomi Barko, "William Inge Talks About *Picnic*," *Theatre Arts*, XXXVII (July, 1955), 67.
25. *4 Plays by William Inge*, pp. vii-ix.
26. "Defector," *Newsweek*, LIX (May 14, 1962), 110. Addressing this point, Inge is quoted as saying, "I was treated as though I had spit on the floor."
27. *Idem*.

28. William Inge, "More on the Playwright's Mission," *Theatre Arts*, XLII (August, 1958), 19.

29. "Candidates for Prizes: 9 Younger Playwrights," *Vogue*, CXXIII (May 1, 1954), 135.

30. *"Picnic:* From 'Front Porch' to Broadway," p. 33.

31. "How Do You Like Your Chopin?" New York *Times*, February 27, 1955, II, 3.

32. *A Loss of Roses*, Bantam Edition, p. vii.

Chapter Two

1. *American Writing in the Twentieth Century*, p. 102.

2. "Talk of the Town," *New Yorker*, XXIX (April 4, 1953), 24.

3. See, for example, John Gassner, *Theatre at the Crossroads*, p. 307, or Gerald Weales, *American Drama Since World War II*, p. 46.

4. William Inge, "The Schizophrenic Wonder," *Theatre Arts*, XXXIV (May, 1950), 23.

5. Richard Maney, "Blackmer's Big Scene," New York *Times*, April 2, 1950, II, 3.

6. "The Schizophrenic Wonder," p. 23.

7. *Idem.*

8. Space does not permit the writer to give any detailed resumé of the critical reception of *Come Back, Little Sheba;* however, the most significant comments on the play are found in the following sources: Phyllis Anderson, "Diary of a Production," *Theatre Arts*, XXXIV (November, 1950), 58-59; Brooks Atkinson, "Two Actors," New York *Times*, February 26, 1950, II, 1; William H. Beyer, "The State of the Theatre: Dance, Stage and 'Drama-goes-'Round,'" *School and Society*, LXXI (June 3, 1950), 342-46; Harold Clurman, "A Good Play," *New Republic*, CXXII (March 13, 1950), 22-23; Wolcott Gibbs, "The Dream and the Dog," *New Yorker*, XXVI (February 25, 1950), 68, 70; "New Play," *Newsweek*, XXXV (February 27, 1950), 74; "New Play in Manhattan," *Time*, LV (February 27, 1950), 81; Kappo Phelan, "The Stage," *Commonweal*, LI (March 3, 1950), 558.

9. *4 Plays by William Inge*, p. vii.

10. Quoted in W. David Sievers, *Freud on Broadway*, p. 354.

11. Naomi Barko, "William Inge Talks About *Picnic*," *Theatre Arts*, XXXVII (July, 1953), 66.

12. *An Analysis of the Dramatic Structure in Three Plays by William Inge*, pp. 38-39.

13. For the identification of this theme in the play, see Barko, p. 67.

14. Among the most representative reviews of *Picnic* are the following: Brooks Atkinson, "Inge's *Picnic*," New York *Times*, March 1, 1953, II, 1; Eric Bentley's review in *New Republic*, CXXV (March 16, 1953), 23; Harold Clurman, "Theatre," *Nation*, CLXXVI (March 7, 1963), 212-13; Wolcott Gibbs, "Something Old, Something New," *New Yorker*, XXIX

(February 28, 1953), 65-66; Richard Hayes, "The Stage," *Commonweal*, LVII (March 20, 1953), 603; Walter Kerr's review in *New York Theatre Critics' Reviews, 1953*, p. 350; Theophilus Lewis, "Theatre," *America*, LXXXVIII (March 7, 1953), 632-33; Theophilus Lewis, "Theatre," *America*, LXXXIX (May 2, 1953), 147; George J. Nathan, "Director's Picnic," *Theatre Arts*, XXXVII (May, 1953), 14-15; "New Play in Manhattan," *Time*, LXI (March 2, 1953), 72, 74; "*Picnic:* More Fun," *Saturday Review*, XXXVI (March 7, 1953), 33-34; "*Picnic* Tells Conquest of a Kansas Casanova," *Life*, XXXIV (March 16, 1953), 136-37; "Reviews," *Newsweek*, XLI (March 2, 1953), 84. Mr. Kerr's review is also reproduced in Barnard Hewitt's *Theatre U.S.A., 1668-1957*, pp. 459-61.

15. *4 Plays by William Inge*, p. viii.

16. *Theatre at the Crossroads*, p. 308.

17. Gerald Weales indicates the symbolism with which Inge uses the names of his characters in *Bus Stop*. See *American Drama Since World War II*, p. 48 fn.

18. *America*, XCIII (April 9, 1955), 54.

19. *New Republic*, CXXXII (May 2, 1955), 22.

20. *New Theatre Critics' Review, 1955*, p. 347.

21. Weales, p. 44.

22. Gassner, p. 307.

23. "The Men-Taming Women of William Inge," *Harper's* CCXVII (November, 1958), 55.

24. "New Play in Manhattan," *Time*, LXV (March 14, 1955), 58.

25. "Mr. Inge's Meringueless Pie," *Saturday Review*, XXXVIII (March 19, 1955), 24.

26. "Mr. Inge in Top Form," New York *Times*, March 13, 1955, II, 1.

27. For additional comments on *Bus Stop*, see the following reviews: "Best Comedy of the Season," *Life*, XXXVIII (March 28, 1955), 77-80; Wolcott Gibbs, "Inge, Ibsen, and Some Bright Children," *New Yorker*, XXXI (March 12, 1955), 62, 64, 66-68; Robert Hatch, "Theatre," *Nation*, CLXXX (March 19, 1955), 245-46; Richard Hayes, "The Stage," *Commonweal*, LXII (April 8, 1955), 14; "Love at a 'Bus Stop,'" New York *Times Magazine*, March 20, 1955, p. 59; "On Broadway," *Newsweek*, XLV (March 12, 1955), 99; Maurice Zolotow, "The Season On and Off Broadway," *Theatre Arts*, XXXIX (May, 1955), 21-22, 87-88.

28. Gassner, p. 171.

29. *4 Plays by William Inge*, p. ix.

30. *Idem.*

31. *The Theme of Loneliness in Modern American Drama*, pp. 16-26.

32. Gassner, p. 171.

33. *Ibid.*, p. 172.

34. "A Question of Reality," *Commonweal*, LXVII (March 14, 1958), 616. For additional commentary on *The Dark at the Top of the Stairs*, the following are especially noteworthy: Harold Clurman, "Theatre," *Nation*, CLXXV (December 21, 1957), 483-84; "The Dark at the Top of the

Stairs," *Theatre Arts*, XLII (February, 1958), 20-21; Patrick Dennis, "A Literate Soap Opera," *New Republic*, CXXXVII (December 30, 1957), 21; Tom F. Driver, "Hearts and Heads," *Christian Century*, LXXV (January 1, 1958), 17-18; Wolcott Gibbs, "The Crowded Stairway," *New Yorker*, XXXIIII (December 14, 1957), 83-85; Henry Hewes, "Light in the Living Room," *Saturday Review*, XL (December 21, 1957), 27; "New Play in Manhattan," *Time*, LXX (December 12, 1957), 42, 44; "The World of William Inge," *Theatre Arts*, XLII (July 1958), 62-64.
35. "The Men-Taming Women of William Inge," p. 56.

Chapter Three

1. *4 Plays by William Inge*, p. vi.
2. "Defector," *Newsweek*, LIX (May 14, 1962), 110.
3. *American Drama Since World War II*, p. 45.
4. *Idem.*
5. Tom Driver notes some of these in "Wanted: Fresh Air," *Christian Century*, LXXVII (January 2, 1960), 15-16.
6. "Theatre," *Nation*, CLXXXV (December 2, 1957), 483.
7. "Going Left With Fortune," *Theatre Arts Monthly*, XIX (May, 1935), 328.
8. *The Theatre in Spite of Itself*, pp. 238-40 *passim.*
9. "Theatre," *Nation*, CLXXXV (December 2, 1957), 483.
10. "Natural Affection," *Theatre Arts*, XLVII (March, 1963), 59.
11. "Tour de Force," *New Yorker*, XXXVIII (February 9, 1963), 66.

Chapter Four

1. Jerry Leroy Crawford, *An Analysis of the Dramatic Structure in Three Plays by William Inge*, p. 1, fn. 1.
2. Random House Edition, p. vii.
3. Charles M. Barrett, *William Inge, The Mid-Century Playwright*, unpublished master's thesis in drama, University of North Carolina, 1957, p. 25.
4. Originally published in 1950 in *New Directions in Prose and Poetry XII*, pp. 528-34.
5. Barrett, p. 47.
6. *Ibid.*, p. 51.
7. *The Dramatization of Female Frustration in Four Plays by William Inge*, unpublished master's thesis in drama, San José State College, 1960, p. 94.

Chapter Five

1. Josephine Murphey, *The Nashville Tennessean Magazine*, September 20, 1953, pp. 7-17.
2. "Theatre," *America*, LXXXIX (May 2, 1953), 147.

Notes and References

3. "The Most Promising Playwright," New York *Times,* July 23, 1950, II, 1.

4. "Defector," *Newsweek,* LIX (May 14, 1962), 110.

5. *Dramatic Heritage,* pp. 11-12.

6. *William Inge, The Mid-Century Playwright,* p. 104.

7. "Pity the Dumb Ox," *New Republic,* CXXVIII (March 16, 1953), 22-23.

8. New York *Times,* March 22, 1953, II, 3.

9. See for example Robert Brustein's "The Men-Taming Women of William Inge," *Harper's,* CCXVII (November, 1958), 52-57, or Adrienne E. Reeves' unpublished master's thesis, *The Dramatization of Female Frustration in Four Plays by William Inge,* San José State College, 1960.

10. "The Multiversity," *Harper's,* CCXXVII (November, 1963), 42.

11. *Theory and Technique of Playwriting,* pp. 252ff.

Selected Bibliography

PRIMARY SOURCES

A. *Plays*

Bus Stop. New York: Random House, 1955. Also published in *Theatre Arts*, XL (October, 1956), 33-56.

Come Back, Little Sheba. New York: Random House, 1950. Also published in *Theatre Arts*, XXXIV (November, 1950), 60-88.

Dark at the Top of the Stairs, The. New York: Random House, 1958. Also published in *Theatre Arts*, XLIII (September, 1959), 34-60.

Farther Off From Heaven. Unpublished play, 1947.

4 Plays by William Inge. New York: Random House, 1958. This volume contains Inge's first four Broadway productions: *Come Back, Little Sheba; Picnic; Bus Stop;* and *The Dark at the Top of the Stairs.*

Glory in the Flower. Published in *24 Favorite One-Act Plays,* edited by Bennett Cerf and Van H. Cartmell. New York: Doubleday and Company, Inc., 1958.

Loss of Roses, A. New York: Random House, 1960. Also printed as Bantam Paperback J2490, New York, 1963; and in *Esquire*, LI (January, 1960), 138-44.

Mall, The. Esquire, LII (January, 1959), 75-78. See also *Summer Brave and Eleven Short Plays,* below.

Natural Affection. New York: Random House, 1963.

Picnic. New York: Random House, 1953.

Splendor in the Grass [Scenario]. New York: Bantam Books, 1961.

Summer Brave and Eleven Short Plays. New York: Random House, 1962. This volume contains these plays in the following order: *Summer Brave; To Bobolink, For Her Spirit; People in the Wind; A Social Event; The Boy in the Basement; The Tiny Closet; Memory of Summer; Bus Riley's Back in Town; The Rainy Afternoon; The Mall; An Incident at The Standish Arms;* and *The Strains of Triumph.*

To Bobolink, For Her Spirit. Published in *New Directions in Prose and Poetry,* XII (1950), New York: New Directions. See also *Summer Brave and Eleven Short Plays,* above.

B. *Thesis*

David Belasco and the Age of Photographic Realism in the American Theatre. Inge's unpublished master's thesis in English, George Peabody College for Teachers, Nashville, Tennessee, 1936.

Selected Bibliography

C. Selected Articles

"Concerning Labels," New York *Times*, July 23, 1950, II, 1.
"How Do You Like Your Chopin?" New York *Times*, February 27, 1955, II, 3.
"More on the Playwright's Mission," *Theatre Arts*, XLII (August, 1958), 19.
"Most Promising Playwright," New York *Times*, July 23, 1950, II, 1.
"*Picnic*: From 'Front Porch' to Broadway," *Theatre Arts*, XXXVIII (April, 1954), 32-33.
" 'Picnic': Of Women," New York *Times*, February 15, 1953, II, 3.
"Playwright, His Mission, The," United States Information Service, 1956.
"Schizophrenic Wonder, The," *Theatre Arts*, XXXIV (May, 1950), 22-23. 22-23.

SECONDARY SOURCES

To date, no full-length study of William Inge has been published. The following works, however, contain significant material relevant to the author and his work.

A. Theses

BARRETT, CHARLES M. *William Inge, The Mid-Century Playwright.* Unpublished Master of Arts thesis in Drama, University of North Carolina at Chapel Hill, 1957. A well-researched study which contains especially valuable material on *Farther Off From Heaven*, this thesis treats also the Broadway productions up to and including *Bus Stop*.

CRAWFORD, JERRY LEROY. *An Analysis of the Dramatic Structure in Three Plays by William Inge.* Unpublished Master of Arts thesis in Speech and Drama, Stanford University, 1957. Although lacking in biographical information about Inge, this study of *Come Back, Little Sheba*, *Picnic*, and *Bus Stop* is valuable in demonstrating "Inge's constant control over his action . . . resulting in a unified whole."

REEVES, ADRIENNE ELLIS. *The Dramatization of Female Frustration in Four Plays by William Inge.* Unpublished Master of Arts thesis in Speech and Drama, San José [California] State College, 1960. This paper attempts to expand on Brustein's "The Men-Taming Women of William Inge."

B. Books

BROUSSARD, LOUIS. *American Drama: Contemporary Allegory from Eugene O'Neill to Tennessee Williams.* Norman: University of Oklahoma Press, 1962. Broussard claims that Inge "comes closest to a discipleship with [Eliot], with his interest in the commonplace."

CLURMAN, HAROLD. *Lies Like Truth.* New York: The Macmillan Company, 1958. In this book, Clurman, who directed Inge's *Bus Stop*, is concerned primarily with *Picnic* which he calls "a solid success."

Current Biography, Who's News and Why. Vol. XIV, No. 6. New York: H. W. Wilson Company, 1953. This source contains basic biographical material.

DUSENBURY, WINIFRED L. *The Theme of Loneliness in Modern American Drama.* Gainesville: University of Florida Press, 1960. The consideration in this book, which is one of the most provocative studies in modern American drama, is limited to *Come Back, Little Sheba* "in which a woman's loneliness because of her personal failure is presented."

GASSNER, JOHN. *Theatre at the Crossroads.* New York: Holt, Rinehart and Winston, 1960. Gassner gives specific attention to *The Dark at the Top of the Stairs,* which he considers a "group play . . . excellently orchestrated." He considers *Come Back, Little Sheba* Inge's "most considerable work."

HEWITT, BARNARD. *Theatre U.S.A., 1665-1957.* New York: McGraw-Hill Book Company, 1959. The editor presents Mr. Clurman's review of *Come Back, Little Sheba* from *New Republic* and Mr. Kerr's review of *Picnic* from the New York *Herald Tribune.*

KERR, WALTER. *The Theatre in Spite of Itself.* New York; Simon and Schuster, 1963. Mr. Kerr is concerned with *The Dark at the Top of the Stairs* and with *A Loss of Roses.*

KUNITZ, STANLEY J. and VINETA COLBY, eds. *Twentieth Century Authors.* (First Supplement.) New York: H. W. Wilson Company, 1955. The article on Inge contains basic biographical details.

LAWSON, JOHN HOWARD. *Theory and Technique of Playwriting.* New York: Hill and Wang, 1960. While Lawson does not deal specifically with Inge, invaluable general comments on dramatic structure are directly applicable to him.

SIEVERS, W. DAVID. *Freud on Broadway.* New York: Hermitage House, 1955. Sievers deals with *Come Back, Little Sheba* and *Picnic,* both of which he calls Naturalistic dramas. He quotes Inge as saying that "Freud has deepened and expanded man's own awareness of himself."

THORP, WILLARD. *American Writing in the Twentieth Century.* Cambridge: Harvard University Press, 1960. Thorp deals only briefly with Inge, commenting on his Realism.

WEALES, GERALD. *American Drama Since World War II.* New York: Harcourt, Brace and World, Inc., 1962. Weales briefly treats all of Inge's major plays through *A Loss of Roses,* setting them in interesting and valuable historical perspective. The study is intelligent and provocative in relation both to Inge and to modern American drama generally.

C. Articles

This section is representative rather than exhaustive. For further listings regarding reviews of individual plays, see "Notes and References."

Selected Bibliography

ANDERSON, PHYLLIS. "Diary of a Production," *Theatre Arts*, XXXIV (November, 1959), 58-59. This article traces the course of *Come Back, Little Sheba* from the presentation of the typescript to the Theatre Guild until opening night nearly a year later.

ATKINSON, BROOKS. "Inge's *Picnic*," New York *Times*, March 1, 1953, II, 1. Commends Inge for keeping this play "terse and pertinent."

————. "Mr. Inge in Top Form," New York *Times*, March 13, 1955, II, 1. Atkinson reviews *Bus Stop* with favor, calling it "fresh and illuminating."

————. "Two Actors," New York *Times*, February 26, 1950, II, 1. Atkinson notes the contrapuntal design of the Marie-Turk romance in *Come Back, Little Sheba*.

BALCH, JACK. "Anatomy of a Failure," *Theatre Arts*, XLIV (February, 1960), 10-13. Gives biographical insights in regard to Inge and the failure of *A Loss of Roses*.

BEYER, W. H. "The State of the Theatre: Dance, Stage, and 'Drama-Goes-'Round,'" *School and Society*, LXXI (June 3, 1950), 342-46. Beyer comments on Inge's underwriting in *Come Back, Little Sheba*.

BRACKER, MILTON. New York *Times*, March 22, 1953, II, 1, 3. One of the earliest major biographical articles on Inge.

CLURMAN, HAROLD. "A Good Play," *New Republic*, CXXII (March 13, 1950), 22-23. Clurman defines a "good play" and fits *Come Back, Little Sheba* to his definition.

"Defector," *Newsweek*, LIX (May 14, 1962), 110. This article tells of Inge's disenchantment with Broadway theater and his captivation by Hollywood.

DENNIS, PATRICK. "A Literate Soap Opera," *New Republic*, CXXXVII (December 30, 1957), 21. In calling *The Dark at the Top of the Stairs* a soap opera, Dennis stipulates that Inge's "soap is of the best French-milled quality."

DRIVER, TOM F. "Hearts and Heads," *Christian Century*, LXXV (January 1, 1958), 17-18. Driver regards *The Dark at the Top of the Stairs* as Inge's best play since *Come Back, Little Sheba*.

GIBBS, WOLCOTT. "The Crowded Stairway," *New Yorker*, XXXIII (December 14, 1957), 83-85. Gibbs comments on Inge's almost infallible ear and controlled style. He calls *The Dark at the Top of the Stairs* "well worth seeing."

————. "The Dream and the Dog," *New Yorker*, XXVI (February 25, 1950), 68, 70. Gibbs calls *Come Back, Little Sheba*, "a peculiar mixture of effective realism and psychological claptrap."

————. "Inge, Ibsen, and Some Bright Children," *New Yorker*, XXXI (March 12, 1955), 62, 64, 66-67, 68. Gibbs notes the "simplicity of design and . . . clean competence of execution" in *Bus Stop*.

HAYES, RICHARD. "A Question of Reality," *Commonweal*, LXVII (March 14, 1958), 615-16. Hayes notes that *The Dark at the Top of the Stairs* "is full of the pleasure of recognition."

————. "Only Connect . . .," *Commonweal,* LXXI (January 2, 1960), 395. Hayes describes *A Loss of Roses* as "muddled private pathology."

HEWES, HENRY. "Oedipus Wrecks," *Saturday Review,* XLII (December 19, 1959), 24. Hewes writes of *A Loss of Roses* with great restraint; calls Inge's characters uninteresting.

LEWIS, THEOPHILUS. "Theatre," *America,* LXXXIX (May 2, 1953), 147. Lewis expresses his dismay at Inge's being awarded the New York Drama Critics' Award for *Picnic.*

McCARTEN, JOHN. "Tour de Force," *New Yorker,* XXXVIII (February 9, 1963), 66, 68. McCarten accuses Inge of trying in *Natural Affection* to be a "junior-varsity Tennessee Williams."

MANEY, RICHARD. "Blackmer's Big Scene," *New York Times,* April 2, 1950, II, 3. Tells of the strain of the seventeen-minute drunk scene in *Come Back, Little Sheba* on Sidney Blackmer, who portrayed Doc.

MURPHY, JOSEPHINE. "Broadway's White Hope," *The Nashville Tennessean Magazine,* September 20, 1953, pp. 7-17. A generalized, highly optimistic assessment of Inge.

————. "The Birth of a Playwright," *The Nashville Tennessean Magazine,* September 27, 1953, pp. 10-12. Gives information concerning Inge's emergence as a playwright of note.

STANLEY, KIM. "Kim Stanley Talks About *Picnic,*" *New York Times,* April 3, 1953, p. 54. Miss Stanley views *Picnic* from the standpoint of an actress in the play.

"The Talk of the Town," *New Yorker,* XXIX (April 4, 1953), 24-25. Gives insights into Inge's childhood and early youth.

"Tender Insight, A Touch of Toby," *Life,* XLIV (January 6, 1958) 74-77. Concerned primarily with *The Dark at the Top of the Stairs,* this article tries to relate Inge's acting in Toby shows with his style of writing.

TYNAN, KENNETH. "Roses and Thorns," *New Yorker,* XXXV (December 12, 1959), 99-103. This unfavorable review calls *A Loss of Roses* fragmentary; classifies it as a "ritual drama."

WILLIAMS, TENNESSEE. Introduction. *The Dark at the Top of the Stairs.* New York: Random House, 1958, pp. vii-ix. Williams relates how he first came to know Inge and the respect which he has for him.

"The World of William Inge," *Theatre Arts,* XLII (July, 1958), 62-64. Essentially a review of the film version of *The Dark at the Top of the Stairs;* the reviewer comments on the wide emotional range of Inge's work.

ZOLOTOW, MAURICE. "The Season on and off Broadway," *Theatre Arts,* XXXIX (May, 1955), 21-22, 87-88. Zolotow is appreciative of Inge's good taste in his presentation of the characters in *Bus Stop;* he calls the play "a most enjoyable evening of dramatic pleasure."

Index

Index